PRECIS IV

American Architecture: In Search of Traditions

Journal of the
Graduate School of Architecture and Planning
Columbia University

Edited by Sheryl L. Kolasinski and P.A. Morton

Editors
Sheryl L. Kolasinski
P.A. Morton

Editorial Board
Sara Hart
Kenneth Kaplan
Richard Kreshtool
Daniel Monk

Faculty Advisor
Michael Mostoller

The editors wish to thank the following students of the GSAP for their help in the production of this issue:
John Keenen
Barbara Laskey
Kathryn Linder
Neill Parker
Dale Peterson
Francesca Rogier
Claudia Russell
Nancy Solomon
Wen Yijin

Special thanks are due to James Stewart Polshek, Dean of the Graduate School of Architecture and Planning and Arlene Jacobs, Assistant Dean for Administration. For their advice and comments, we wish to thank Max Bond, Chair of the Division of Architecture, and Robert A.M. Stern, Suzanne Stephens, Peter Forbes and Susan Cohn.

Cover Design
Donna J. Wax

This issue is made possible by contributions from:
The Graham Foundation

Abramovitz, Harris, Kingsland
Cain, Farrell and Bell
Davis, Brody and Associates
Ulrich Franzen/Keith Kroeger and Associates
Gruzen and Partners
Gwathmey and Siegel Architects
Johnson/Burgee Architects
Kohn Pederson Fox Associates
Mitchell/Giurgola Architects
I.M. Pei and Partners
James Stewart Polshek and Associates
Prentice and Chan, Ohlhausen
Wank Adams Slavin Associates

And individual contributions by:
Andrew Alpern '64
George W. Clark '47
Duk Wun Rhee '72
Francine M. Rothenberg '75

ISBN: 0-8478-5373-X
Printing and typography by Morgan Press, Inc.

Distributed by:

RIZZOLI
NEW YORK

RIZZOLI INTERNATIONAL PUBLICATIONS, INC.
712 Fifth Avenue, New York, NY 10019

4 Contributors

5 Introduction
Sheryl L. Kolasinski and P.A. Morton

6 Forum: Promising Directions in American Architecture

18 The Development of a California Style:
Regionalism and the Spanish Colonial Revival
in Southern California 1890-1930
Theresa Gordon Beyer

22 American Buildings and Early Modernism
Dale Peterson

26 Pragmatism and Provinciality:
Italian Criticism of the American Plan
P.A. Morton

28 From the Introduction to *Design and the Public Good*
Richard Plunz

32 The Contextualism of Eliel Saarinen
Carolyn Senft

36 Foundations: American House Types
Steven Holl

40 Home in America:
Early Alternatives to the Single-Family House
Graham S. Wyatt

44 Formalism Follows Functionalism:
Critical Attitudes Towards
Post-War American Architecture
Sheryl L. Kolasinski

46 From *The Decorated Diagram:*
Harvard Architecture and
the Failure of the Bauhaus Legacy
Klaus Herdeg

48 The Progressive Uses of Tradition
Jon Michael Schwarting

52 First Year Studios
Master of Architecture
Spring 1982

60 Urban Housing for the Eighties:
The High Rise Block with Common Services
Michael Mostoller

64 Single Room Occupancy Housing
Second Year Studio
Master of Architecture
Fall 1981

70 Museum Projects:
Master of Science
Building Design
Second Year Studio
Master of Architecture

82 On Museums
Colin Cathcart

83 Second Year Studio
Master of Architecture
Spring 1982

88 Third Year Studio
Master of Architecture
Fall 1981

100 Third Year Studio
Master of Architecture
Spring 1982

118 Historic Preservation
Master of Science
Spring 1982

120 Urban Design
Master of Science
Fall 1981 and Spring 1982

124 Esquisse: Memorial for the Vietnam Veterans
of New York City

128 Photographic Credits

Contributors

Theresa Gordon Beyer
Master of Architecture 1982

Christine Boyer
Associate Professor of Urban Planning (Historic Preservation)

Colin Cathcart
Master of Architecture 1983

Alan Colquhoun
Professor of Architecture, Princeton University

Stanton Eckstut
Adjunct Associate Professor of Architecture;
Director, Urban Design Program

Kenneth Frampton
Professor of Architecture

Klaus Herdeg
Professor of Architecture

Steven Holl
Adjunct Assistant Professor of Architecture

Sheryl Kolasinski
Master of Architecture 1983

Mary McLeod
Assistant Professor of Architecture

Edward Mendelson
Associate Professor of English and Comparative Literature

P.A. Morton
Master of Architecture 1983

Michael Mostoller
Director of the Master of Science Program in Architecture and Building Design; Adjunct Associate Professor of Architecture

Dale Peterson
Master of Architecture 1983

Richard Plunz
Associate Professor of Architecture

Jon Michael Schwarting
Associate Professor of Architecture

Carolyn Senft
Master of Science in Architecture and Urban Design 1982

Robert A.M. Stern
Associate Professor of Architecture

Graham S. Wyatt
Master of Architecture 1983

Introduction
American Architecture: In Search of Traditions
Sheryl L. Kolasinski and P.A. Morton

For there either was some Tristero beyond the appearance of the legacy America, or there was just America and if there was just America then it seemed the only way she could continue, and manage to be at all relevant to it, was as an alien, unfurrowed, assumed full circle into some paranoia. (From *The Crying of Lot 49* by Thomas Pynchon, New York, 1966)

Today architects are faced with the problem of determining the relationship of the past to present architecture. In this post-modern period, we recognize that although the spirit of modernity distanced contemporary architecture from specific historical ties, we are now reevaluating our connection to the past. But, does the rediscovery of history lead to a recovery of tradition or is the modernists' declared break with history irrevocable? The questions of whether and how traditions can be appropriated or referred to is the subject of this issue of *Precis*.

As yet, we find no definitive answers to these questions. In the absence of a collective theory, some regard the past as a source of images and forms to be mined at will, some find history mute given the constant change and consumerism of modern life, and others affix specific political, economic and philosophical principles to varying degrees of historical appropriation. However, it is clear that this is no longer a neutral issue.

This issue is particularly relevant to American architecture, since the United States is at once a young country without long-standing traditions and the foremost sponsor of the internationalization of culture. If anything, we have a tradition of the new. We revel in the current and novel yet have a history of borrowing, imitating and transforming the traditions of other cultures. If the past can inform American architecture, of what does this past consist?

The articles in this issue of *Precis* describe some of the ways in which tradition has been regarded in America by American and European architects, theorists and critics. The topics include the transformation of received traditions, vernacular architecture, American urbanism, the role of immigrant architects, and European views of American architecture. Contemporary practice is addressed in articles that propose a model for the reintegration of traditions or which comment critically on current or past attitudes toward tradition.

As an extension of our interest in current practice, the Editors and Editorial Board sponsored a symposium in the fall of 1982 entitled "Promising Directions in American Architecture". In this forum, Alan Colquhoun of Princeton, Kenneth Frampton, Mary McLeod and Robert A.M. Stern of Columbia's GSAP, and Edward Mendelson of the Columbia Department of English and Comparative Literature discussed their views of American architecture today. To them, and to all of those who contributed to *Precis*, we extend our thanks.

This publication coincides with a national symposium, entitled "American Architecture: Innovation and Tradition", inaugurating Columbia's new Temple Hoyne Buell Center for the Study of American Architecture. This event, co-directed by David DeLong, Helen Searing and Robert A.M. Stern, promises to focus on many of the same issues which have concerned us. We welcome the founding of the Center as an additional forum for dialogue which reflects the diversity and richness found at Columbia and throughout the architectural community today.

Forum:
Promising Directions in American Architecture

Panel Discussion
Avery Hall
Graduate School of Architecture and Planning
November 29, 1982

Moderator
Edward Mendelson

Participants
Alan Colquhoun
Kenneth Frampton
Mary McLeod
Robert A.M. Stern

Mendelson: This panel has been put together to ask the question, what are the promising directions in American architecture today? The fact that the question is as open as it is reflects the recent, crucial changes in the arts. Twenty years ago there was an orthodoxy and now, for better or worse, that orthodoxy is broken. That does not mean that any one tradition has been supplanted or superseded or discredited. It simply means that the range of possibilities is open; and, with that openness, problems arise.

One can approach the problems in architecture by focussing on the other arts. First, there is the example of the revolution in early music and its performance. Recently, an extensive movement has developed that attempts to perform music of the sixteenth, seventeenth and eighteenth centuries in the styles, and with the instruments, for which that music was originally composed. This means that if you want to perform Mozart or Bach today, you have two choices. Either you can perform it in the way recognized by tradition, the way that has developed over the past hundred years, or you can perform it in a radically different way using old instruments, string instruments strung in the old style, harpiscords, certain kinds of brass instruments without keys and with different styles of articulation. What this means is that those who perform early music in 'authentic' ways are returning to the past but they are doing so by rejecting the very recent past.

The style of performance of Bach of up to twenty years ago—the traditional style—is being turned aside for a different style of performance, one that supposedly existed two hundred years ago. A recovery of the past is done in a way that has been established by modernists, a way that breaks with tradition. Even to go back to the past, you reject the recent and immediate past. Even for those who don't want to be modern, the methods, the assumptions of modernism become part of the landscape.

Another example is in literature where, say twenty or thirty years ago, in the French novel or French criticism, the assumption made by anyone who was willing to show his face in public was that the subject of the novel was its own medium, its own language. It explored what happened to language itself rather than any historical event. It was also assumed that this was a great liberation from past assumptions. The French theoretical magazines that argued this point twenty years ago have now suddenly started coming out with special issues on the historical novels that they were once ashamed to talk about. In doing so, the historical novel is rendered no longer 'innocent'. Critics and novelists recognize that even if you were to write about the historical past, you would see it through the lens established by modern literature, by modern assumptions about the formal independence of the author.

One thing that happens at the end of an international style of modernism is that you begin to substitute a local tradition for an international tradition. In doing so, however, you have learned the international tradition. There is no innocent return, and, at the same time, there is the sense that the return is in some way desirable.

Now, with those issues placed on the table, I will yield ten minutes to Mr. Colquhoun.

Colquhoun: Just to make a point about what Professor Mendelson has said, there is, of course, a tradition of revival as well as a tradition of continuous tradition. That tradition goes right back to the Romans. The Romans revived Greek architecture and Greek art quite consciously from time to time. So one might say that the present tendency for revival is in itself a tradition.

To pick up the question of the other arts raised by Mendelson, I was talking to a friend who teaches music at a university and I asked him how composition was taught in schools of music. I thought there might be some interesting parallels between the sort of confusion that exists in schools of architecture at the moment and what exists in other fields. I had always imagined that there was in music, if not in any other field, a tradition; that is to say that I thought that one learned how to compose in the 'classical' system before one rejected it to go on to something else. Apparently this is not the case. There is, in fact, no formal tradition of composition that is now taught and the effectiveness of the composition is judged entirely on a consensus among faculty and students as to what works and what does not work.

This seems to be exactly the same as in schools of architecture. It seems to have been very much the same ever since around 1940 when the Beaux Arts stopped being taught. I don't think the present situation is essentially different from that. Therefore, I don't think we are in a situation of revivalism. I quite agree with Professor Mendelson that, whatever the problem may be, we are still looking at it from an essentially modern perspective.

Briefly, I find the question before this symposium almost impossible to answer because one really is not aware of any particular direction in which things are going. One might be aware of what direction it ought to go. But certainly, there seem to be no clear clues as to the way in

Left to right: Robert A.M. Stern, Mary McLeod, Edward Mendelson, Kenneth Frampton, Alan Colquhoun

which American architecture is moving at the present moment.

It seems to me, that the difference between now and the post-1920s era is that, in those days, though there was no longer a formal method of teaching, there was a definite ideological program. This ideological program does not exist today. It is the rejection of the 'tradition of the new' as formulated in 1900 or 1910.

One can, however, make a few personal comments about the direction one would like things to go in and, in this, I may well be saying something other people on the panel will disagree with. It seems to me that there are two parallel theories of architecture and I put 'theories' in inverted commas at the moment. One is that architecture should be formally rich instead of formally impoverished; the other is that architecture should in some sense recover a tradition and so become symbolically full of meaning. I see nothing wrong in either of these propositions in themselves, but they often seem to act against each other. We do not enjoy classical architecture (at least I do not enjoy classical architecture), only because it is formally rich, but *primarily* because it is formally coherent. When the chief aim of architecture is formal richness the result seems to very often lack coherence. It seems to be in the direction of ornamental confusion and the absence of meaning, rather than fullness of meaning. This does seem to me a feature of a certain amount of American architecture at the moment. There seems to be no essential difference between a 'Modernist' building which spins meaningless and vulgar ornament on the curtain wall or plays around with the shapes of skyscrapers and, on the other hand, a 'Post-Modernist' building in which every functional difference is made an excuse for some different quasi-historical formal device. Both belong to the same tradition of formalism which really has nothing to do with tradition.

Now, to step out honestly in front, my feeling is that the importance of tradition would lie in what links modern man to a constant tradition of values, and those formal correlations in architecture would be found at a level different from the individual style. It follows that there should be some degree of abstraction. Somehow or other we cannot avoid abstraction and the reason for this is quite clear. There is no longer any genuine, living tradition (that is quite indisputable to me), not only in architecture but in every other art. The only difference between this abstraction and the modernist abstraction would be that it sees architectural values as based on a historical tradition independent of programmatic and technological modernity.

Therefore, if I can state my position in a brief sentence, it seems to me that one can only subscribe at the moment to the negative proposition according to which there is no particular fit between architectural form and architectural content in the old holistic sense. Further than that I do not feel that it is possible for me to go.

Frampton: Today's situation brings to mind a rather strange text which Stanley Tigerman wrote for a catalogue entitled *America Draws.* It featured the work of a number of American architects in the form of their drawings. This exhibition was sponsored by the museum of architecture in Helsinki. In this somewhat wild text, Tigerman made a claim for a new and late liberation of America from the repressive influence of Europe. On another occasion he delivered himself of the witticism that "Post-Modernism is a Jewish movement."

This question as to promising directions today also reminds me of an occasion at the Institute for Architecture and Urban Studies when Paolo Portoghesi was in town to talk about the *Strada Nuovissima* of the Venice Biennale of 1980 from which I had, so to speak, abdicated, at least in the sense that, at one time, I had been invited to contribute a critical piece. After Portoghesi lectured on the *Strada Nuovissima,* I was to make a response. And, during the course of this reply, an unexpected insight came to me. I remarked that "There is a ghost absent at the Post-Modern feast and the name of this absent ghost is Frank Lloyd Wright." This caused a certain consternation. In fact, it caused Vincent Scully to lose his buttons because soon after that he piped up with the statement, "Oh, you are quite wrong about that because Robert Venturi began where Wright left off," which is one of the most absurd and coarse critical judgments I've ever heard in my life. Frank Lloyd Wright is still a taboo topic. Unfortunately for the Post-Modernists (or if you want to call it revisionism or whatever), they cannot talk about Frank Lloyd Wright because, in fact, there was not a reductive bone in his body. His work represents the true American modern tradition. Probably Johnson Wax is the finest piece of American art (not only architecture) realized in the twentieth century.

However, that was in the mid-30s. In the early 70s the following telling and amusing, apocryphal exchange took place between Louis Kahn and Robert Venturi, when they were both invited to submit designs for the Bicentennial Exhibition in Philadelphia. In the process of hanging their

1

drawings—Kahn's in monochrome and Venturi's in brilliant color—at some point Kahn could not bear the contrast any longer and he turned to Venturi and said, "You know Bob, color ain't architecture." There was a pause and Venturi replied, "You know, Lou, a Bicentennial Exhibition ain't architecture either." This exchange gives, I think, a condensed notion, not only of our internal confusion, but also of the kind of briefs which are given by society and the kind of emphasis which is placed on architecture at this particular period of history—I mean the media emphasis.

I feel at this juncture that it is necessary to try and distinguish betweeen reductive criticism and reductive art. It seems to me that the very term, The International Style, is an example of reductive criticism. It was the invention of Messers Hitchcock and Johnson. It was reduction from the very beginning because the International Style (so-called) was, in fact, very inflected, even in 1932. To speak of a style was to reduce its nuanced expression, to package it as some kind of instant modernism which could be readily absorbed by the East Coast in a moment when it suited the ideological purposes of the Establishment to do so. Of course, the Museum of Modern Art was a powerful instrument in this operation.

In an address given in Frankfurt by Jürgen Habermas two years ago on the occasion of the Theodor Adorno prize (an address in which he began by referring to the *Strada Nuovissima* as the quintessence of Post-Moderism in modern culture), he observed that the stress and crisis induced by the modernization of society had not been called forth by modernist intellectuals. These stresses are, in fact, the consequences of processes driven forward by late Western instrumentality, by the communications systems, by the media, by the economy and by techniques of control. Architecture has suffered for quite a while from the impact of the media. I can even see the photograph itself as playing a reductive role in architecture since, as an extension of the Renaissance idea of perspective as distanced vision, photography involves what Heidegger calls 'loss of nearness.' This loss of nearness is in itself one of the problems involved in perceiving and conceiving architecture today. An example of this would be Arthur Drexler's *Transformations* exhibition of 1979, which consisted of roughly some 500 photographs at one shot the building. It was a great public success. "Distracted from distraction by distraction" one might say of this exhibition and the way it was received (and I did say it and Arthur Drexler did not speak to me for quite some time!).

After I wrote that book which caused Robert Stern so much distress [*Modern Architecture: A Critical History*] (in which, since we have been talking of ghosts, of course, he found that I was surely Giedion's). I was advised by Dalibor Veseley of a text by Paul Ricoeur entitled *Universal Civilization and National Culture,* which appears in English in a paperback called *History and Truth.* I have since been greatly influenced by what Ricoeur has to say, above all by the distinction he draws between culture and civilization. He says that there are no developing countries (and it is quite clear that we are all developing countries, even the United States) that are going to forego the benefits of civilization, which means, of course, they are not going to renounce atomic weaponry, nuclear power, modern medicine, electronic communication techniques, advanced distribution methods, and even the panoptic aspects of cybernetic control. Ricoeur asserts that the challenge which faces the species in the last quarter of the twentieth century is whether it can still sustain the presence of the identity-giving aspects of culture, at the same time as it maintains and enjoys the benefits of civilization. I think this is a challenge that not only affects architecture but other cultural fields as well.

Architecture, however, is not like the other arts inasmuch as outside the humanist tradition (and I think there is a great deal of architecture that lies outside the humanist tradition) architecture is not as much involved with representation as with presentation; that is to say, with a kind of ontological immediacy. The condition of this immediacy is threatened and eroded directly by the media. It was Abraham Moles who observed that the monuments of Europe are being worn out by Kodaks and I think that this aphorism fairly characterizes the situation we are in today. Architecture is clearly no longer an avant-garde business. It is more of a rearguard affair and I think that some form of critical regionalism which, without falling into sentiment, tries to mediate between culture and civilization is, perhaps, the only direction to go in any national culture, not only American.

McLeod: Although I share both Ken Frampton's and Alan Colquhoun's hesitation about literal prescription, I am going to put myself somewhat on the line tonight and suggest two trends that I find rather encouraging in contemporary architecture, or I should say, the environment more generally. The first emerges from the recent work of several environmental sculptors. The constructions of

2. *Field Rotation, Park Forest
South, Illinois, Mary Miss,
1981*

2

Mary Miss are among the finest examples. The second involves the projects of a group of younger architects, perhaps best represented by the drawings of an American architect now teaching in England, Peter Carl. Though of different media and not always considered architecture, if architecture is narrowly conceived as built, functional form, both approaches embody an attitude towards meaning which accepts architecture's abstract dimension, but without denying the possibility of association or external suggestion.

With regard to sculpture, I might remind you of a talk that Philip Johnson gave a couple of years ago at Columbia on architecture. His paragon was Alice Aycock's recent work—simple wooden structures that are essentially abstract but resonate with images and associations, none of them literal but still filled with suggestion. And, although I disagree with the rest of his talk (and, in general, with his kind of historical eclecticism which is based on little more than personal whimsey), I am deeply sympathetic with this choice. Like Mary Miss's work, Aycock's sculpture deals with the ambiguities of environmental form; the elements of enclosure, columns, walls, boundaries, are in themselves rarely specifically referential. Of primary interest are the relationships between the pieces. But neither are the constructions intended (as in the architecture of Peter Eisenman) to exist in total autonomy. They accept the fact that form exists in the world. As in music, the meaning or associations are often difficult to grasp or convey in verbal terms, but this fact does not negate the persistence of memory or the sensations of corporeal experience.

With regard to architecture, I would cite, on the one hand, the work of those individuals who deal explicitly with the associational quality of abstract form, such as Peter Carl, Lars Lerup and Daniel Libeskind, and on the other hand, the work of those designers exploring a more minimal vocabulary such as Mark Mack, Andrew Batey and some of my Columbia peers including Steve Holl and Lauretta Vinciarelli. Common to the designs of these admittedly disparate figures is what I would call a rejection of a 'correspondence' notion of meaning: that forms can literally be read as words; that representation, given changes in technique, architectural audience, and values, is still possible as a literal enterprise. In contrast to the literal historicism of Post-Modernism, there is an understanding that architecture does not always refer first to something else. In other words, the articulation of a split between a physical element and an idea sometimes becomes problematic in an abstract medium. Designation does not always follow recognition; it is recognition. Thus, to propose a building as a specific code or message, as was the purported objective of many of the recent Chicago Tribune Competition entries, risks being trivial.

These younger designers engage in what might be considered a more ambitious and realistic undertaking (admittedly with varying degrees of success and realization thus far): to create an architecture that expresses the ambiguity between abstraction and association, silence and suggestion that is intrinsic in architecture's nature. Their designs generally emphasize the more architectonic dimensions of building—walls, structure, proportion, composition—which, though evocative of ideas, rarely are conceived as an explicit cultural message. In contrast again to the so-called Post-Modernists, they freely employ many of the formal discoveries of the Modern Movement: asymmetry, layering, transparency, collage, though without the stylistic imitation of the New York Five architects, for instance. These devices, I would argue, do not obliterate the potential meaning of the work, but rather provide opportunities to explore the very multivalence and multiplicity of meaning originally decreed in *Complexity and Contradiction*. Without literal reference, they permit a reading of the complexity of modern experience, the simultaneous assertion of hierarchy and its questioning. Yes, in prosaic hands we are sometimes left with a kind of Miesian, empty, universal space, but in the evocative studies of Carl's urban places or Lerup's houses, a new potential for expression emerges. They are not grandiose enclosures or spaces, but the question one must pose is: should they be?

Many of the historicists discuss similar themes. Multiplicity, multivalence, complexity, richness are words we hear again and again. Yet, the formal prescriptions, apart from ornament, tend to be reductive: for instance, static space and symmetry. In the struggle to communicate a message, they are often forced to simplify and overstate their images. One of my French contemporaries, himself a Post-Modernist, referred to several recent American projects as Disneyland Classicism. Perhaps that's our national style.

Finally, I would like to add a few remarks about polemics and social message. In a recent address Fredric Jameson characterized one of the predominant features of post-Modernism as an end to polemics, an end to manifestos. This is certainly not the case of Jencks or his fellow traveler sitting close to us. But I do feel that it is generally true of the architects and sculptors I have been talking

3   4

3. *Project for My Body, Gibney Farm, Pennsylvania, Alice Aycock, 1972*
4. *Twenty Seventh Street at Eighth Avenue, Fashion Institute of Technology Master Plan, Design Collaborative (Piero Sartogo and Jon Michael Schwarting), 1982*

about (with the possible exception of Mack and Batey who have recently espoused a kind of neo-primitivism). For the most part, these individuals reject the simplicity of Modern Movement dogma but also the equally simplistic viewpoint of those who want to return to the past. They offer no easy prescriptions like "form follows function" or "imitate past styles and the *Zeitgeist* will take care of itself" (a phrase I have heard around here.) Rather they are anti-instrumental, whether the proposed method is stylistic or functional in intention. Likewise the relationship to politics and social ideals has altered. In contrast to the utopianism of the Modern Movement architects or the categorical rejection of that by the subsequent generation (who offer in its place a kind of neo-populism that frequently appears to be little more than a eulogy to the *nouveau riche*), many of the individuals that I have mentioned acknowledge architecture's potentially critical role. If not messianic neither are they passive. Without simple answers, they recognize a responsibility to consider social implications. As an example, one might cite a group of architects currently meeting together in New York, which includes some Columbia faculty: Lauretta Vinciarelli, Michael Schwarting, and Michel Kagan, as well as a number of other architects such as Bernard Tschumi, Deborah Berke, and Joan Ockman.

A last point to these remarks is simply the question, why American architecture? Certainly the Modern Movement itself made suspect the nationalism which characterized such exhibitions as the *Deutsche Werkbund* or *Arts Decoratifs.* I most willingly endorse regional distinctions when they are the legitimate outgrowth of local education, cultural traditions, production practices, materials, or climate, but given the universal dissemination of architectural books and journals, the broad marketing of commodities, and frequently homogeneous economic pressures, I believe that such distinctions are increasingly less important, at least along national lines. Sometimes the differences between Chicago and California or New York and California are as important as those between America and France or even America and Europe. Our own faculty and student body includes numerous foreigners; we sponsor European summer programs. Such situations are not unique, but speak to the intermix in architectural currents whether they be functionalist, historicist, typological, or involve attitudes toward meaning.

Stern: All sides have been taken by everyone, if not always to my advantage. If I am to be a traveller, I always want to go first class. I don't know how Jencks travels.

I am most impressed with what Professor Jameson is said to have said. Because I do believe that the meaning of Post-Modernism is that there is an end to these silly, pointless polemics of dividing people up as though everyone had to have one point of view. That is really the trick of it. Mary is very critical of other points of view but she has a point of view; other people here have a point of view, yet not too many have been put on the table.

I thought the purpose of this occasion was to analyze or to speculate on the conditions in American architecture today. While I don't think that American architecture is necessarily unique among the world's architectures, it is in some degrees self-sufficient, and its many component parts are each worth commenting on. In particular, I am very impressed with the power of the provincial to make art, to communicate, to make art meaningful to other architects and to the public in general. There seems to be some feeling around here tonight that the public, if given something it likes, is being pandered to, that an architecture that has a popular following is something I believe Professor Frampton has called conciliatory consumer kitsch (presumably all spelled with 'k's').

I believe that there is a power to being specific. I believe there are general rules and general feelings in architecture. But I also believe that what makes architecture interesting is how the local cultures, which usually grew up relatively spontaneously and are called vernacular, interact with the wider ideals. In that case, I am very encouraged by American architecture today.

However, if I were to list the architects of interest I think I would come up with rather a different list from Mary McLeod's. She has listed a group of younger architects who are pursuing one strand of many, the lone strand of a continued international culture which is an expression of the provincial aspect of our American situation. America has been afflicted with a colonial complex for a very long time. We should not suffer from a colonial complex. We should enjoy the colonial complex. We are colonials to the entire world, and everybody comes from at least two places, which makes this a fascinating place.

We should seek out in our architecture, as in everything else, the distinctions and the commonalities. That is what makes American literature so fascinating in our time. The Jewish novel, the Irish novel, you have it. Only in our architecture, it seems to me, do our leading builders and

5. Loyola Law School, Los Angeles, California, Frank Gehry and Associates

5

writers shrink from this problem as they tirelessly search for an architecture rooted in the timeless banalities of 'significant space' and eternal values of 'support' and 'supported' etc. (as if anybody could care any more about these issues in and of themselves). That is the instrumentality.

To list what is happening in architecture, I would start with my own home town, New York, and I would point to the return, the revitalization, of the long-cast-asunder tradition of congestion, of high density buildings, of buildings that have poetry of type, a self-proclaimed poetry of advertisement, because if Raymond Hood is intriguing to us then, so must be Cesar Pelli or Philip Johnson. We can't have it both ways. We can't admire Raymond Hood because he is safely dead and not admire the contemporary manifestations.

I would admire, on the other end of the spectrum, someone like Frank Gehry on the West Coast because he has taken that local tradition of the shack and he has reinterpreted it. He has also revitalized and carried forward the individualist tradition in our architecture. Professor Frampton is worried about Frank Lloyd Wright. I was at that confrontation; I think he misrepresents Professor Scully, but that is another subject entirely. (I have been known to misrepresent for polemical purposes also.) But I do think that Frank Lloyd Wright is hard to come to terms with precisely because he is a great individualist. He did not operate out of a tradition. So, Gehry is an individualist and is equally fascinating.

For the first time in my professional life since I was a student, there is a vitality of practice, a diversity of points of view that cuts across ages, that cuts across places, that accommodates European trends which are, of course, "superior" (we are Americans, we know where we stand), and allows us to wallow with deep pleasure and some profit in our own provincial, misguided, consolatory, peculiar ticks. This vitality and diversity is the Post-Modern condition. It has nothing to do with overthrowing one thing for another. It has to do with the narrow-minded, single search that began with the International Style polemic and continued through the institutionalization of Modernism through the 50s and 60s. It is no longer dominating or crippling our search for a richer or more meaningful architecture (to use those cliché terms) at last and once again we may have an architecture that is internationally viable because it has about it a provincial basis.

Mendelson: Can you give some specific prescriptions for students of architecture to use in finding a tradition, or the meaning in tradition?

Colquhoun: I don't think it is a matter of easy prescriptions. It would be if one was in a direct tradition like the Beaux Arts tradition where, in fact, there were a set of rules which were reasonably easy to follow and, therefore, it was very easy to distinguish the very brilliant students from the not so brilliant students. I think that situation simply does not exist today. While one can guardedly talk about the importance of a tradition, this does not mean that one is offering a certain set of prescriptions as existed in the past.

Frampton: I don't know whether it is so impossible, and I suppose everyone has their own way of approaching such an issue. To me, one of the most erosive tendencies in architecture today is its reduction to scenography. The strongest potential for architecture to resist becoming merely scenographic is a return to the poetics of construction and to what can be called the tectonic value of the constructional and structural elements. So I think that that certainly this is an aspect which can be stressed both in architectural education and practice.

The other thing that can be emphasized is the idea of place creation as a general cultural strategy. All evidence to the contrary, Robert Stern and I live in different worlds. I cannot forget for a second the extent to which the basic premises of our dominant mode of production and consumption have a marked tendency to render all architecture irrelevent. It seems to me that, without falling into a hopeless negativity, what architecture still possesses is its intrinsic capacity to make places because, in general, given the spontaneous processes of our industrial society, places are the last thing that actually come into being.

McLeod: I would like to raise one issue. I think the meaning of tradition has to be clarified. I don't think one can talk in the United States about a Jewish architecture or an Irish architecture, just as it's difficult for one to talk about Jewish music or Irish music. Occasionally, one can tell the ethnic background of the composer from his music, but it is by no means a given.

6

6. Johnson Wax Administration Building, Racine, Wisconsin, Frank Lloyd Wright, 1936-39.

Tradition is not always an issue of literal representation. It can also involve construction techniques and compositional relationships. The ordering structure or method of design can be as important to tradition as referential imagery.

Stern: Every building is studied by historians as a partial explanation of a circumstance. It is not only the architect's education or his belief in one compositional mode vs. another that is interesting when we study buildings, but also learning about who the people were who commissioned them. It is perfectly possible to build for the middle class or for the capitalist or whoever and to incorporate that fact into the building. I am convinced that McKim, Mead and White and the architects of that generation who produced extremely solid buildings and wonderful places, also kept in mind the fact that they were working for a certain clientele at a certain time. There was cultural xenophobia and many other kinds of xenophobia at that time in New York and they tried to reify (as the current buzz word goes) certain values through their buildings by deciding to use the Roman orders as opposed to the Georgian vocabulary which they used in other circumstances.

Being an architect: You make it all sound so negative and boring. I think architects have tremendous power to help understand what the clients need, to make a stab at it. Most of us fail, but we take a stab at it. I am convinced of our capacity to draw upon all that is meant by the term "architectural traditions" including the Modernist tradition, to express or to further the expression of building program, to make places and monuments and icons. Such a traditional approach is an extremely powerful and positive aspect of our architecture today.

I think, Ken, there is a complete confusion in your argument. On the one hand you favor place-making but make a wholesale dismissal of scenographics. Scenographic architecture has a long tradition going back at least as far as Inigo Jones, and many of the most successful places have, in part, been made out of a conscious act to mold a setting against which the action of human life will be played. To return to an architecture based on the poetics of tectonics is to reduce architecture once again to nuts and bolts as though the rest would have to be provided by other people. I cannot accept that.

Frampton: I mean by tectonic, not technique, but the elevation of elements to a much more significant level than just technological efficiency. Above all, I do not mean nuts and bolts. I do mean Carlo Scarpa. I do mean Frank Lloyd Wright, certainly as his contribution is manifest in Johnson Wax.

One thing that is worth remarking on is the fact that clients themselves have changed and one shouldn't deceive oneself into thinking that the clients are not different. The client that built Rockefeller Center in the 30s had, in my view, a vision of the destiny of capitalism in relation to this country which was quite specific. The client that built Rockefeller Center after the Second World War was virtually anonymous, 'the government of nobody', a committee which simply produced so much floor space and a reductive building. This occurred not only because modern architecture provided them with a convenient envelope in which to accommodate the operation, but also because the captains of industry had ceased to have any ideas about what was America's or capitalism's destiny. They had shifted into the gear of international monopoly capitalism which unfortunately, as we all know, does not understand the meaning of patriotism. So we see that the client has indeed fundamentally changed. The big client, at least, is different and, clearly, we are talking about the big client if we are talking about high density in New York.

Stern: You cite Rockefeller Center, which was completed over twenty years ago, as though it was a relevant discussion point. Why don't you talk about the buildings that are being built today? Let us try and live in the present. There are many small-time entrepreneurial types who have a great romance with capitalism. They've made a lot of money. George Klein loves to build "self-important buildings and hire fancy architects to express something special. A man like De Butts, the former president of AT&T, is a man who rose up through the ranks of capitalism—a new organizational type. He had a vision strong enough to pull that building through for better or for worse.

I think you are so negative. You have a romance about New York in the 1920's, a romance about this place and that place from the past which does not allow you to approach what is happening now on its own terms...

We only study the representative models of excellence. We neglect or we ignore or we put on the back burner things that did not work out. Things are more complex in

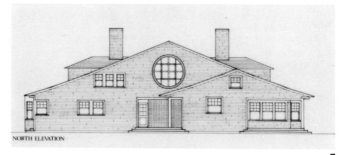

7. *Residence at Farm Neck,
Martha's Vineyard, Massa-
chusetts, Robert A.M. Stern*

NORTH ELEVATION

7

our time, but I think if architects give up and say, "there is no possibility; everything must be nothing," then, of course, we will have been abandoned. We have been abandoned. We are only just once again not being abandoned.

You say our architecture is being killed by the media. The media is not the enemy of architecture. The fact that architecture is the subject of media investigation for the first time after twenty or twenty-five years of neglect is, I think, significant.

Colquhoun: I agree with a certain amount of what Robert has said, but I think he should admit that there is a certain distinction between what he calls regionalism and the kind of eclecticism that exists today in architecture, which I don't think is regionalism in quite the sense he tries to make out. I think Robert's idea is somewhat nostalgic, somehow connected with the nineteenth century, when there were, in fact, different sub-groups within society who had quite strong ideas of what buildings should look like and what they represented which would constitute a sort of regionalism or a sort of localism or whatever. I don't think today that really exists. I think the differences between different styles insofar as they are carried out by architects are largely the choice of the individual architects. I don't think they have anything to do with an existing set of sub-cultures, as you presented them: the Jewish, the Irish, etc. (**Stern:** I was referring to literature, not architecture.) I think it is a myth. I think Ken is right. I do think there is a distinction between today's eclecticism and the eclecticism of the nineteenth century. Today's eclecticism is largely a matter of advertising. The desire for a certain thing is created by advertising. There may be nothing wrong with this, but it is not the same as nineteenth century eclecticism. That is the point I want to make.

But I would like to say one more thing. I find it highly amusing that both Robert and Ken should find themselves on the same side of the fence. Regionalism was the invention of the Romantic movement and of the Gothic Revival in the nineteenth century. And so was the idea of tectonic value of structural elements. So, in the end, Robert and Ken are both being nostalgic about exactly the same thing.

McLeod: I agree with what Mr. Colquhoun just said. I have trouble also with the regional nostalgia I find in Ken's remarks, as well as those of Robert. Ken seemed to be postulating some kind of Heideggerian stance, suggesting

we can retrieve some basic notion of place and being. This seems problematic to me given the monopoly capitalism we just talked about. I really think there are very few regional cultures that emerge as legitimate manifestations of continuous tradition. The other point that I would like to raise concerns the nature of stylistic choice. I have a hard time distinguishing Robert Stern's position from the historical eclecticism of nineteenth century. I wonder if he would distinguish it at all.

Stern: I don't know that I believe in progress. I did not mean to give that impression. I thought you quoted me much more accurately before: "Let the *Zeitgeist* take care of itself." If we are interested today in Georgian and tomorrow we are interested in Gothic let's not brood about it. Let's just do it, and it will be our Georgian and our Gothic or our modern.

McLeod: That choice, that sort of freedom is incredibly different from a regional vernacular.

Stern: I did not mean to advocate just a regionalism in that narrow sense, that you do shingles in certain places, and so forth. But I could defend it in relationship to Alan's remarks. I do think there are responsibilities that architects have because they are educated to interpret certain circumstances even though the traditions in a spontaneous way may not actually prevail. . . . I don't think it is possible to discuss architecture only on the abstract level. I think that is too limited a view. I think any discussion here or in our studios is always much richer when it tries to discuss both the abstract or ongoing values of architecture and the specific representational devices that the designer has marshalled to make his point, to make his building, to make his design.

Mendelson: Can we continue this discussion of regionalism and its possible uses and methods as relates specifically to the American situation?

Colquhoun: I can only respond to that as a European who is essentially a visitor to America. When somebody talks to me about American regionalism, I just laugh. I can drive

8　9

from New York for three or four hundred miles and to me there is no change at all: the same McDonalds, the same this, that and the other. The landscape changes (very slowly, incidentally, much more slowly than in Europe, which may have something to do with the lack of regionalism in America) but one certainly is not aware as a European of any apparent and strong regional characteristics. I am not saying they don't exist, but their presence is not predominant.

On the contrary, the interesting thing is that in Europe there is still very definitely a regionalism. Even within European countries you still have considerable regional differences from one place to another—for instance, in food.

In spite of this, in Europe as in America, there is a general universal culture which is superimposed on this regionalism. It really is true, I think, to say that the idea of a modern regionalism is completely absurd with television and radio and vast systems of transport. Somehow or other we have to face this situation.

What I can't quite understand is Robert's view that we should accept all the goodies of modern society, but we should also accept this kind of regionalism which to me is something that really doesn't exist. It is a figment of the architect's imagination and the imagination of somebody who has a nostalgia for an architecture that is still making figural statements. It seems to me that whatever we think modern architecture should be, it can't be exactly like it was in the late nineteenth century when there were these various traditions which actually existed, craftsman-like traditions where the builders did things in certain ways and the architects responded to that. This is where regionalism in architecture genuinely existed, in the craft of building. Present regionalism, it if exists at all, exists in the imagination of architects and of the advertisers who want you to travel somewhere.

Frampton: That criticism is directed almost as much to me as it is to Robert, and I would like to make some observations. I think that to sustain a rich culture of architecture which has depth and nearness is rather difficult in this period of history. Nonetheless, I think it can be attempted.

By critical regionalism I do not mean folklore, I do not mean vernacular. I do not mean a simple-minded imaginative effort to fall back into some hypothesized vernacular or nostalgia. I do mean, however, the effort that could be made in schools or in cities or in districts to create

(however short-lived) a kind of local culture which would have some direct, living relevance to the immediate circumstances of the society. As I tried to indicate by evoking the arguments advanced by Ricoeur, this is not to advocate some kind of hermeticism. It must mean to use progressive techniques of production, as well as time-honored means of fabrication, and then to try to mediate or synthesize the one with the other. I think that out of this it is possible, under certain circumstances, to develop a regional culture.

McLeod: I certainly think there are areas of the United States where there is a regional culture, such as Santa Fe, and believe that in designing one should consider regional conditions, climate, technique, tradition, whatever. But I don't think examining those things is going to lead very far in making architecture in this day and age . . .

To think one is going to dig out of a suburb in Maryland, as opposed to one on Long Island, some notion of regional culture is as much of a dead end as Leon Krier's approach.

My next point is that the real centers of architecture in the United States these days tend to be California, New York, Chicago; in fact, those areas that are the most cosmopolitan, the most diversified in terms of ethnic background, nationality, etc.

Stern: First, I am going to apply for a grant and take Alan Colquhoun for a tour around the United States. I do think that 400 miles is not very far in the U.S. There is a problem of scale that I think was the cause of your remarks.

But, more seriously, I think it is Mary that I am most concerned about. I think you have a very limited view of the term 'regionalism' which admittedly, like every term, is loaded.

I think New York has a regional style, character. It is cosmopolitan; that is part of its special character. I think that New York's skyline, New York's texture, New York's attitude to streets and buildings is unique and calls forth an architectural response and many different scales that distinctly define New York. When I was speaking of regionalism, I wasn't thinking of a suburb of Maryland or New York. That is exactly the opposite of regionalism. That is the kind of consumerist place that we all abhor as a debasement of ideas.

I may have misunderstood you, Ken, but it seems to me you implied that an architect could make a region. If

10. House at Stabio, Switzerland,
Mario Botta, 1981

10

that is what you said, then I think I would part company with you because I think a region is something that can only grow out of the interaction of all the forces of society. Whenever someone like Charles Moore (whose work supports my arguments) has worked outside an actual region—as at Kresge College—he fails because the buildings are not enough on their own—do not have sufficient density—to spontaneously generate an entire new life that one thinks of as a region or even as urban. I do think that one can respond to a region. I think that is the obligation of an architect. I do think we quarrel because, for example, of your advocacy of the so-called rational work of the Swiss which seems to me anti-regional although you argue for it as a critical regionalism. I can't understand that. It looks to me like it could be built anywhere, anytime in the last forty years. It may be accomplished or not on an individual basis, but it is definitely not regional in the way I understand the term.

Frampton: This business of critical regionalism is hard to make specific. I think that the work of the Swiss—of Mario Botta in particular—does amount to a kind of critical regionalism. In fact, critical regionalism is not without its own pathos and I can easily provide you with an example of that. I think that houses of Botta's, invariably built in concrete block and usually assuming a prismatic form, either in the form of a barn or silo-like mass and set in the landscape (as the agrarian types alluded to) are charged with a certain pathos. Even more pathetic is the fact that the vista from the primary fenestration of these houses is designed in such a way as to give a view of the landscape before it was virtually destroyed by local speculation and German migration. Nevertheless, I think that it embodies a critical quality first, because it speaks of a lost harmony and second, because it has its own evident vitality. It uses steel fenestration, it uses standard, rationalized techniques of production, it will occasionally use antique forms of crafted production, such as the polished plaster fireplace surrounds in the otherwise modern farm complex built by Botta in Ligrignano.

I don't really think one can approach the creation of architecture today without applying a great deal of subtlety and sceptical questioning. I don't think one can simply jump on the Philip Johnson bandwagon and have an orgy of style and say, "Boy, if you do it well, nothing else matters," or that even if you embody your images in curtain wall that is also OK. Between Helmut Jahn and Philip

Johnson there is not much to choose because in the end both are dedicated to rock bottom production. Jahn talks about 'populist machinism', but dressing up multistoried buildings as though they were halfway between Art Deco objects and giant Wurlitzers doesn't really make for culturally resonant architectural form. If one cannot approach the discipline with greater subtlety than that, one might as well just go and do something else.

Stern: Ken, you wouldn't have liked the Woolworth Building either for the same reason. It is a very American phenomena. It is the genius of the place. As a critic, I think you have to accept it.

McLeod: What I worry about is the instrumental quality of Bob's recommendations—as if there is enough regionalism to make architecture. I am certainly not against a consideration of regional factors, but that is very different from proposing regionalism as a specific style or way to design.

How do you design for a suburb if there is no regional context? What do you do about a problem like Kresge College? My basic point is that there isn't very much that we can rely on as a given to use as a method of designing. I think there is a difference between contextual consideration and a proposal of regionalism as a possible formula solution for American architecture.

Stern: There are other ways to use tradition besides the local tradition, which is what regionalism implies. You can make a new place as Jefferson did: the university, based on the tradition of architecture which he borrows and interprets and forges something new.

Colquhoun: You cannot do now what Jefferson did in 1800.

Stern: Why not?

Colquhoun: Times have changed, Bob.

11

Stern: Times had changed in Jefferson's time too. And he was trying to do something. I don't understand why one cannot.

Colquhoun: Because with Jefferson there was a tradition of understood meanings in connection with classical architecture. The Enlightenment situation was one in which there were generally understood associations of ideas with classical architecture. These do not exist today.

Stern: I think they exist for some.

Colquhoun: They exist for the architects, perhaps.

Mendelson: Who, then, is the audience for your architecture?

Stern: I think they exist for more people than the architects. My experience as an architect now is that the general public—the relatively educated public who communicates with architects and commissions architects—knows a lot more about architecture. These buildings have far more associative and intellectual values for those people than the architects give them credit for. After all, the generally educated person out of Columbia College or Princeton or any solid place of higher learning has studied the history of architecture, has been imbued through humanities classes with the values of the Renaissance and so forth. I think he actually values those works far more than architects give him credit for. I think it is part of the negative reaction of modernism to assume that these things no longer have meaning. They do. They do have meaning to the culture in general. People go to the National Gallery in Washington and to the East building and get the messages very clearly from those two buildings and those two formal languages and those two sets of intentions. They draw their own conclusions as intelligent people. I think you underestimate the meaning of this system. They understand only too well what modernism (and this is the Jencksian argument, I realize) has come to mean. Their associations and understandings of how the forms evolved, why they have been perpetuated in certain sectors of the world and certain sectors of the economies of countries is only too explicit, and they absolutely reject it, not just out of taste, but out of

real understanding of what these forms have come to mean.

Colquhoun: I wouldn't deny at all that people have the notion of different architectures or that styles having different meaning, but they are not the same meaning that Jefferson saw in 1800. Jefferson wasn't someone who existed in a vacuum. He existed in a very strong culture which was shared between America and France and England at that time. All that I am saying is that those conditions, the conditions which produced the Lawn at Charlottesville, are not the conditions that exist today. We can understand, we can interpret, we can respond to this in our own ways, but we know we will never know whether we are responding in the exact same way as he did. You would say it does not matter and I would say, in that case, if you are not sure that our response is different, how can you see Jefferson as an example?

Stern: Because it did not matter that he did not get it right from the models on which he was basing it. He imagined what Palladio's vision was or what ancient Rome was like. The capacity to design buildings, to make places in architecture, is the capacity to imagine a condition. You bouy up your imagination in many different ways, as many as possible, because if you do, it is bound to be more successful, to speak to a wider audience. People go to the Lawn. You go there and I go there and we look at it and say it is a beautiful place and we have associations: You love the brick. There are many different reasons why people admire the Lawn. Only specially educated people understand that the buildings were meant to be didactic and that they grew out of a certain culture of the Enlightenment. We can extend that language as the nineteenth century extended it, as some few architects of the twentieth century did and we can continue to extend that language. Its meanings change, grow and reduce depending on all kinds of circumstances, but they are there. You cannot say, as I think you are saying, that you cannot do it because you obviously can and it is being done.

Colquhoun: The whole argument is a *Zeitgeist* one. My criticism of your remarks would be that you tend to regard peoples' reactions to buildings or peoples' decision to use certain styles with certain meanings as being totally detached from ideology.

Stern: I didn't say that.

Colquhoun: I am not taking Ken's position that the only possible solution is a kind of extension of modernism. I don't believe that. What I am saying is that I don't believe in your position either: that somehow we can go on doing the same thing.

McLeod: I basically think that as well. One of my problems with what Bob is proposing is that I believe that it is part of the responsibility of the architect to be conscious of how those meanings have changed. One thing that struck me very much was a comment of Max Bond's that columns and porticos in the South suggest slavery to him. I think we must deal with the fact that associations have changed and that sometimes regional references don't just mean the continuation of a classical and humanist tradition; they can also suggest colonialism and a kind of monumentality that is inappropriate. As architects, we need to be extremely conscious of and responsible about those associations.

Audience question: As part of the style issue—whether we use Gothic or classical or modern—how can we deal with the problem of finding people to build things properly? The quality and craftsmanship of things built today is so inferior.

Colquhoun: I think it is a very important point. I think it has to do with Mary's or Ken's point about scenography. In America one notices a sort of disjunction between what the building is trying to look like and what the building really is. We haven't touched on the ontological problem.

There is a problem, I think, with the lack of craft in modern buildings and the fact that modern buildings make their effect by scenographic methods in which the impression or fact of permanence doesn't have any say at all. I think this is a fact of modern life that one has to live with. To me this opens the intriguing question as to whether we are dealing with the problem of abstraction which is what I mentioned before and to what extent this implies an architecture of scenography or something else. To me it is an open question.

Audience question: A lot of the examples you gave about looking at architecture are personal. One of the issues in design reviews in terms of our own work is how much of architecture is personal, how we look at it, or contextual. Are we to make our buildings contextual without showing the architect's hand?

Frampton: I don't think you can do something consciously and then also pretend you are doing it unconsciously. A conscious act will manifest itself. It shows a certain confusion and debility in society when [there is a fear] of making a conscious act which has to do with its own period of history. Some kind of limit has to be set on the whole contextual aspiration. If one starts to think exclusively in instrumental terms, i.e. of how am I going to make the drawings pretty?, or how am I going to make the building pretty?, or how am I going to sell this and be a success?, then surely an argument is taking place at some kind of level, but not on one that should detain us here for two hours.

It seems to me that the question of context, of how you mediate the new object in relation to the old and what it adds creatively to the old object involves some act of creation rather than a mere reflex. The kind of attitude which takes the view that whatever one adds to the existing context is bound to be worse than what is already there is totally negative. On the other hand, if one takes a more aggressive approach to this issue, one simply has to give up the idea that any kind of immediate gratification is going to take place, that everybody is going to walk by and think that the building is just wonderful. This is an absurd notion. I think no architecture except architecture that existed before industrialization, that is to say an architecture that is almost an anthropology, has this kind of closeness of fit.

McLeod: I think all of us are against an instrumental approach. It is obviously a very complex art and you can't just prescribe "go look at certain buildings." It is an interweave of functions. One of our roles as teachers is, we hope, to make you conscious of all these variables and processes. Undoubtedly, some of us would stress tectonic qualities and others, more representational qualities. Underneath this are some very strong principles concerning what we believe as teachers. I think to ask for a formula is impossible and reductive of the nature of architecture itself.

The Development of a California Style: Regionalism and the Spanish Colonial Revival in Southern California, 1890-1930
Theresa Gordon Beyer

1. Gas Station, Westwood, 1925
2. Mission Inn, Arthur Bennett Benton, Riverside, 1902-1931

1

2

Architectural histories of the twentieth century have usually dismissed the so-called Spanish Colonial Revival along with the other period revivals that flourished in the 1920's. But the stylistic developments of this period in Southern California were uniquely able to meet the needs of their time and place: the romantic desire for a history and the search for an architecture adapted to its climate, an aesthetic that emphasized simplicity without sacrificing a certain pretentiousness, and building configurations adapted to the casual California life-style. By the 1920's, it became *the* favored style for almost every building: from mansions to humble cottages, from gas stations (*1*) to cathedrals.

The roots of the Spanish Colonial Revival lie in the closing decades of the nineteenth century. The American Centennial and national exhibitions, such as those at Philadelphia (1876) and Chicago (1893), fostered a feeling of pride in America's achievements. Magazines such as *American Architect and Building News, The Brick Builder,* and *Pencil Points* were founded at this time, and through the publication of measured drawings of

American Colonial buildings they encouraged an appreciation of early American architecture.

This nationalistic period coincided with the rapid growth of California as a region. The population of Los Angeles, for example, doubled every ten years between 1880 and 1930. A growing sense of regional pride was manifested in many forms. The beauty of the landscape was celebrated by the Eucalyptus School of painters. The romantic Spanish past was popularized in the 1884 best-selling novel, *Ramona*. A number of general interest magazines which became boosters for all things Californian began publication. For disseminating popular ideas about architecture the most important of these were *Land of Sunshine,* (founded in 1894), *Sunset* (1897), and *California Southland* (1918). In 1915, the Panama-Pacific Exposition in San Francisco and the Panama-California Exposition in San Diego celebrated the achievements of the region.

The nationalistic American Colonial Revival did not become prevalent in California until the 1930's; instead California tried to develop a regional style, separate from the tradi-

*A. An Aesthetic of Contrasts
The Spanish Colonial Revival satisfied two seemingly contradictory aesthetic desires: one for simplicity, and one for ostentation.*

The varied and interesting designs never infringe upon the necessary blank spaces which are as vital and yet as difficult to handle as the proportions of a facade or the placing of its various openings in rhythm and harmony.

"Spanish and English Colonial Homes in California," California Southland, *no. 25, Jan. 1922, p. 10. A*

tions of the rest of the country. (*A*) By the 1890's, the growing appreciation of the old Spanish missions, and the movement to preserve them, inspired an architectural style of California that recognized its existing monuments.[1] The late eighteenth and early nineteenth century missions were admired for their simplicity, dignity, "organic" quality, and adaptation to the local climate and building materials. However, few of the Mission Revival buildings managed to retain these qualities intact when adapting the forms of these large ecclesiastical buildings to modern secular uses and late Victorian eclectic building forms. There were exceptions: the romantic train stations in the center of almost every town; the ultrasimplified buildings of Irving Gill; and the crazy quilt ramblings of the Mission Inn in Riverside. (*2*)

As California architects and their clients became more educated and more travelled, their tastes became more sophisticated; by the late 1910's, they wanted buildings that were historically convincing. The naive quotations of the Mission Revival could not supply the pretentious and erudite image that was desired, so architects

3. *First Congregational Church,*
   Myron Hunt and Elmer Grey,
   Riverside, 1912
4. *Lobero Theatre, George Washing-*
   ton Smith, Santa Barbara, 1922-24
5. *Santa Barbara County Court-*
   house, Mooser and Company,
   Santa Barbara, 1929

3   *4*   *5*

invented a past for California by looking instead to the buildings of Mexico and Spain. Churrigueresque and Plateresque ornament, typically limited to the main entrance, porch or tower (*3*), became popular. Here, the San Diego Exposition buildings of 1915 by Bertram Goodhue were very influential. This version of the Spanish Colonial Revival became most popular for churches, commercial buildings and the larger residences.

Almost concurrent with the Churrigueresque influence was the creation of a more informal style based on the vernacular forms of Southern Spain. This was largely the inspiration of George Washington Smith of Santa Barbara, whose studio-residence of 1916 was based on the simplified forms of the Andalusian farmhouse.[2] This version of the Spanish Colonial Revival became the standard image of Southern California in the 1920's. Informal picturesque massing allowed easy adaptation to different sites and functions. Limited ornament gave the style a modern look and appealed to developers who could suggest a Spanish image with only stucco walls, an

arched window or door and a few tile-topped parapets. Fewer larger buildings were built in this mode, but among the notable exceptions were the Lobero Theater (*4*), the County Courthouse (*5*), the Paseo shopping arcade and the Biltmore Hotel, all in Santa Barbara.[3]

In the middle 1920's, many architects began to reject this somewhat archeological approach. (*6*) They expressed a desire to develop a "California" architecture or style, that would contain the best of the two traditions: "The romance of the Mediterranean with the charm of the English Colonial."[4] Architecturally, this meant that the siting emphasized public display in the front yard; front porches became more common. Interior halls appeared in addition to or instead of cloisters around the patio. Wood shake roofs became common even in houses that were otherwise Hispanic. Norman farmhouses and Tudor cottages were melded with the Spanish hacienda.

One of the most successful modes to develop out of this trend was the Monterey Revival. (*7*) Based on the nineteenth century buildings of the American settlers in Hispanic Cali-

fornia, Monterey Revival houses were symmetrical two-story structures with shutters, whitewashed walls and a balcony across the entire front of the second story. The street facades projected a more "American" image while the back, focussed on a patio or terrace, was often more Hispanic. Direct copying of Spanish types became more frowned upon; for example, while the 1923 by-laws of the garden suburb of Palos Verdes required white wall surfaces and red tile roofs for most of its neighborhoods, they specifically stated that historic styles were not desired.[5] This "California" style was the last phase of the Spanish Colonial Revival proper.

Throughout the period of 1890-1930 persuasive arguments were used to justify the choice of the Spanish Colonial Revival. These arguments ranged from the sentimental to the practical. The persistence of nineteenth century romantic thinking (*B*) was probably the greatest factor in the success of the Spanish Colonial Revival. The success of this argument is evident in its widespread use in advertisements and boosterizing literature. The romantic image of neighborhoods with Spanish architecture

B. The Romantic Justification
Spanish history was sentimentalized and articles about life under Spanish rule appeared virtually every month in regional general interest magazines from the 1890's through the 1920's.

> We feel that we have wandered into another century or become part of an old time poem. This is a bit of Old Spain, transported here on a Magic Carpet, and then turning to ruin and decay like most fairy gifts.

Adele Sterns Wing, "The Mission at San Juan Capistrano", Land of Sunshine, *August 1895, p. 111.*
B

6

7

was furthered by the use of Spanish place names, fiestas and the like. The romantic argument seemed natural and obvious, as did the climate argument. (*C*)

Charles Lummis was one of the first to marshall the arguments for a Spanish Colonial Revival, in particular those based on the Mediterranean climate analogy. In a series of articles in *Land of Sunshine,* he argued for thick walls, whose time-lag insulation would keep the house cool in the summer and warm in the winter;[6] for deep, south-facing verandas, things of "Beauty and sense"[7]; for passive solar design; and for the patio, a lawn within the house, "Every room opens up on it, and every member of the family is joyed and benefitted by it."[8] For Lummis, it was the plan and its logical adaptation to local conditions that was the most important feature of the style he was promoting; the romantic aspects of Spanish ornament and image were secondary.

The patio became the typical feature of the California house. It was included in some form in any Mediterranean style house that was large enough to enclose one (*8*), and was usually suggested in one that was too small, either with a walled entry or a back terrace. Even many Tudor, Norman and Georgian houses of the period included a patio in at least a rudimentary form. Public buildings found many inventive ways of including them: as outdoor reading rooms in libraries, as shopping arcades in commercial buildings, or as enclosed public gardens in courthouses and city halls.

The patio was useful, not only as a place that took advantage of the climate, but also as a place that could be adapted to different social functions. Two different housing types centered on patios became important in California in the 1920's: the single family dwelling and the shared apartment court. The first was the "Ideal American House"[9] for the increasingly prevalent nuclear family, while the second served some common California lifestyles: those of the single person, the childless couple, the retiree.

As the nuclear family became the fundamental unit of American life, it demanded more self-sufficiency. The patio was a place for the children to play away from the "herd in the street."[10] It became the California

equivalent of the hearth, the focus of the family, and as such it represented the security of the family. The patio was also important for outdoor entertainment; it suggested the intimacy and informality of partaking in family life.

Court housing, on the other hand, was a way of providing the image of family life. Entrances to the private units were from a semi-public patio (*9*) which was attractively landscaped to suggest the patio of a large Spanish hacienda. Balconies or small walled patios attached to each unit were often included adjacent to the public patio, while service functions were generally relegated to the back. The inhabitants had most of the advantages of a large garden; light, air, and beauty, without the responsibility for its care.[11]

Ultimately, the Spanish Colonial Revival was almost too successful; people tired of it. It seemed too reminiscent of feudalism for egalitarian America.[12] By the 1930's, California's position as a region apart was well established. With the Depression, regionalism was no longer the compelling force it had been. *Architectural Digest,* published in Los Angeles, was

8. House on Berkeley Street, Wallace Neff, Pasadena, c. 1925
9. El Greco Apartment, Pierpont and Walter S. Davis, Westwood, 1929

C. The Climate Justification

Because of the salubrious climate, many Southern California towns had their beginnings as winter resorts. Many settlers, including not a few architects, came for their health.

> Tradition and sentiment...recognized the architecture of Spain as appropriate to our California climate... but eventually the influence of the Mediterranean Sea, so like our Pacific, is proving the factor.

Advertisement for the Austin Murphy Company, California Southland, *Dec. 1918—Jan. 1919, p. 3.*

C

8

9

almost exclusively illustrated with Spanish Colonial Revival buildings in the 1920's; in the next decade it was dominated by the American Colonial Revival. The shortage of money and the high cost of labor meant that even the relatively simple Spanish Colonial Revival became too expensive to build. The growing popularity of Modern architecture (which the simplified forms of the Spanish Colonial Revival may have helped to make more palatable) marked the decline of the style. When architects were no longer willing to practice traditional styles, only the inaccurate and shoddy builders' versions remained, giving the traditional styles a bad name.[13]

Despite new influences on architectural style, the urge to build within the Spanish/Mediterranean vocabulary is still very strong in Southern California. Towns like Santa Barbara that have continued to appreciate their Spanish downtown have passed ordinances requiring new structures to harmonize with the old ones. Red tile roofs and stucco walls continue to be favorite materials for new development, especially for shopping centers and condominiums. A large part of the success of the style is due to the

flexibility of its parts. Roofs could be sloped or flat. Patios could be shared or private. Walls could be stucco on wood framing or fireproof concrete. Plans could be progressive or traditional. Ornament could be elaborate or nonexistent. And yet, despite all of the possible variations, a common image, that of the romantic Mediterranean, could be projected. In a time when we are beginning to appreciate once again the value of ornament and tradition, these buildings can teach us a great deal.

[1] Harold Kirker, *California's Architectural Frontier,* San Marino, 1960, pp. 120-130.

[2] David Gebhard, *George Washington Smith, the Spanish Colonial Revival in Southern California,* Santa Barbara, 1964, unpaged.

[3] David Gebhard, "The Spanish Colonial Revival in Southern California, (1895-1930)", *Journal of the Society of Architectural Historians,* vol. 26, May 1967, pp. 131-147.

[4] Reginald Johnson, "The Development of a True Californian Style", *California Southland,* no. 87, March 1927, p. 9.

[5] Charles H. Cheney, A.I.A., "Where Poor Architecture Cannot Come, Palos Verdes Estates, California", *Western Architect,* 1928, p. 75.

[6] Charles F. Lummis, "The Lesson of Adobe", *Land of Sunshine,* vol. 2, no. 4, March 1895, pp. 65-66.

[7] Charles F. Lummis, "The Grand Veranda", *Land of Sunshine,* vol. 3, no. 2, July 1895, p. 67.

[8] Charles F. Lummis, "The Patio", *Land of Sunshine,* vol. 3, no. 1, June 1895, p. 13.

[9] "Santa Barbara", *California Southland,* no. 103, July 1928, p. 126.

[10] Arthur Bennett Benton, "The Patio", *Land of Sunshine,* vol. 7, no. 3, August 1897, p. 108.

[11] Stephanos Polyzoides, Roger Sherwood, James Tice, *Courtyard Housing in Los Angeles, A Typological Analysis,* Los Angeles, 1982.

[12] "Spanish and English Colonial Homes in California: The Work of Marston and Van Pelt, Architects", no. 25, January 1922, p. 10.

[13] Jonathan Lane, "The Period House in the 1920's", *Journal of the Society of Architectural Historians,* vol. 20, December 1961, pp. 1969-178.

American Buildings and Early Modernism
Dale Peterson

*1. Pacific Coast Borax Co.,
Bayonne, N.J., 1897-98*
*2. Addition to Pacific Coast Borax
Co., 1902*

1

2

In the late nineteenth century, American architecture began to influence work being done in Europe[1]. In the 1890's H.H. Richardson was an inspiration for the development of National Romanticism in Scandinavia, and during the first decade of the new century Frank Lloyd Wright's work became well known through the publication of the Wasmuth portfolio in Germany. Yet perhaps the most lasting American influence on architecture in this century came not from the work of well-known American architects, but from those photographs of American industrial buildings, published by Walter Gropius and Le Corbusier, which helped create the "functionalist" visual vocabulary of the Modern Movement. As a lasting image of functional architecture, these photographs froze in time a particular style of industrial construction which had only recently been developed and which would shortly be replaced as technological and economic developments continued. Had these photographs of American grain elevators and factory buildings been of structures built ten years earlier or only a few years later, the image would have been very different and their influence on twentieth century architecture might have been altered.

The pace of change in industrial construction technology quickened in the latter part of the nineteenth century, paralleling the rapid growth of American industry and its increasing urbanization[2]. For most of the century, American industry had been located, not in the major cities, but in rural areas where power could be obtained by damming streams and installing water wheels. In this setting it was natural that mill construction developed using relatively unsophisticated techniques and materials which could be obtained locally, including stone for exterior walls and heavy timbers for the inner frame and flooring. American factory builders did not turn to British factory building techniques which required cast iron for framing and brick arched floor structures. Although cast iron began to be used at mid-century for facades and some interior framing in urban buildings, mill construction remained in use for most large industrial buildings, with only such minor refinements as the substitution of brick for stone in exterior walls. This use of brick allowed for an increase in window area and also led to the use of thickened piers between the windows, changing the character of the exterior from solid wall with punched openings to a frame-like structure with brick and glass infill.

This change from heavy exterior walls to a more grid-like frame was accelerated by the development of reinforced concrete construction. In the 1890's, engineers on

3. *Grain elevator*
   Gropius's unretouched version
   Deutscher Werkbund Yearbook *1913*
4. *Grain elevator*
   Le Corbusier's retouched version
   L'Esprit Nouveau *1920*

both sides of the Atlantic developed different systems for the economical construction of buildings combining the compressive strength of concrete and the tensile strength of steel[3]. The Hennebique system was patented in France in 1892 but did not come into widespread use in the United States. Its complexity made it difficult to build with American labor which was both less skilled and more highly paid than in Europe.

More economical methods were devised by the American pioneer of reinforced concrete, Ernest L. Ransome, an engineer and builder. Even before 1890, Ransome had constructed buildings using a mixed construction of concrete floors and iron columns, and in 1897 he built one of the first all concrete factory buildings, the Pacific Coast Borax Refinery in Bayonne, New Jersey. Though it was built entirely of concrete, Pacific Coast Borax looked like a stone masonry building, with heavy walls punctured to provide small windows. This was quickly to change however, for between 1900 and 1902 Ransome patented a new system of reinforced concrete construction in which the floor slab was slightly cantilevered beyond the column line, forming a belt course around the building which was used to support window sills and lintels. The exterior walls no longer carried the weight of the building and it became possible to open very large areas of the walls to windows, creating large daylit factory space. With the cost of steam for heating low and the cost of electricity for lighting high, it was advantageous for the building owner to use as much daylight as possible despite the consequently large heat loss. Ransome's new techniques spread quickly, and several large complexes built under his patents were completed by 1905. The change in Ransome's work can be seen in Figures 1 and 2, both showing the Pacific Coast Borax Refinery. Figure 1 shows the 1897 building with its heavy stone-like walls. Figure 2 shows an addition built before 1907 under the new Ransome patents, in which the large areas of glass and grid-like facade can be seen.

At the same time similar technological changes were occuring in the bulk storage of grain[4]. The mechanical principles for raising grain in grain elevators had been developed before 1850, but the early wooden elevators were plagued by frequent fires. By the 1890's, elevator operators had tried brick, tile and steel in a search for greater strength and safety from fire. Concrete was first tried in an experimental grain bin built in 1900 in Minneapolis by the entrepreneur Horace Peavey. Although concrete proved to be the most expensive way to build a grain bin, its initial cost was offset by dramatically reduced fire insurance premiums, and soon

3

4

5

concrete became the standard material for large terminal elevators, including the complexes built in Buffalo after 1906.

The technological changes which led to the introduction of reinforced concrete construction in industrial buildings and storage silos at the turn of the century and their rapid proliferation by 1910 are an interesting part of the history of American building technology. But the place of these buildings in the broader history of architecture is assured by the fact that they were photographed here and published in Europe within a few years of their construction, at a time when many in Europe were looking for new forms of architectural expression, free from the educated sophistication of Europe.

Walter Gropius was the first in Europe to publish photographs of American industrial buildings. In the *Deutscher Werkbund Yearbook* of 1913 he published, along with his article "The Development of Modern Industrial Architecture," fourteen photographs of industrial buildings from the Americas. Of these, nine are storage silos and five are concrete frame industrial buildings; nine are said to be in the United States, two in Canada, and three in South America. The photographs of elevators are taken from angles which emphasize the geometrical simplicity of their form, ignoring the complex mechanical equipment needed to lift the grain while focusing on the grouped pure cylinders of the storage bins. Gropius is drawn to these images by this simplicity of form which he compares to an ancient untainted sensibility:

The compelling monumentality of the Canadian and South American grain silos, the coal silos built for the

large railway companies, and the totally modern workshops of the North American firms almost bears comparison with the buildings of Ancient Egypt[5].

Gropius admires these buildings not for their sophisticated technology or design, but because they give evidence of an unsullied and primitive aesthetic sense.

(The) American builders have preserved a natural feeling for large compact forms fresh and intact. Our architects might take this as a valuable hint and refuse to pay any more heed to fits of historical nostalgia or other intellectual considerations under which European creativity continues to labor and which stand in the way of true artistic naivete.

The final phrase, "true artistic naivete," is revealing of both Gropius's ideals in architecture and his perspective on American culture. Gropius's search for a natural and naive building art leads him to the American industrial engineer, who assumes the role of Noble Savage, able to create form without recourse to a false sentimentality or an over-sophisticated sensibility.

This admiration for the elemental qualities of American industrial buildings was repeated by Le Corbusier, who published photographs of grain elevators and reinforced concrete industrial buildings in the articles in his magazine *L'Esprit Nouveau* which were later collected and published in *Vers Une Architecture* of 1923. In the section titled "Mass" Le Corbusier used photographs of grain elevators, many of which are the same as those published by Gropius eight years earlier. Le Corbusier was not as convinced as Gropius that the elevators were wholly untainted by artificial sensibility, for he found it necessary to alter the photographs that he had received from Gropius, removing decorative details and context which detracted from the elemental purity of the images[6].

In the accompanying text Le Corbusier returns to Gropius's thesis of the naive sensibility of the American engineer, but with more emphasis on the effect obtained by engineers in buildings such as grain elevators composed of pure geometric solids.

Not in pursuit of an architectural idea, but simply guided by the result of calculation (derived from principles which govern the universe) and the conceptions of a living organism the engineers of today make use of the primary elements and, by co-ordinating them in accordance with the rules, provoke in us architectural emotions and thus make the work of man ring in unison with universal order[7].

In the later section titled "Surface" he argues for geometrical solutions to problems of modern construction.

6. *Grain elevator published by Le Corbusier in* L'Esprit Nouveau, *1920.*

The accompanying illustrations of American concrete frame industrial buildings show facades with a grid-like geometry derived from the modular nature of large scale construction and rational engineering calculations, with windows and doors placed "in accordance with the necessities of their destined use." Here we find themes which were reflected throughout the work of Le Corbusier—the use of rational geometry as an ordering device and the expression of function.

The European fascination with American industrial buildings continued through the twenties. As late as 1928 Erich Mendelsohn's *Amerika* was published in Berlin, with just over a hundred photographs of buildings in America. Mendelsohn's emphasis was on the new American image of the skyscraper, but he included nine photographs of grain elevators. Some of the structures are the same as in Gropius's photos, shown by Mendelsohn with alterations and additions which had been made in the intervening decade and a half.

Looking back at these European views of American industrial construction, we find a source of images for what modern architecture should look like, with simple geometric solids, gridded facades and large expanses of glass. In the name of functionalism, these images were applied to a whole range of building types far afield from their sources in industrial construction. These borrowed images eventually returned to America in the late twenties and thirties, but with a new context and with new meaning as part of the new visual vocabulary of modernism.

The early modernists looked across the Atlantic in their search for new form, sensing that it was necessary that the new form grow from an aesthetic sensibility untainted by sophistication, a sensibility which they detected in the pragmatic products of the American engineer. This search for an untutored naivete lead to the admiration of American reinforced concrete industrial structures of the first decade of the century, a period when developments in the economy and in technology led to large scale building in this new material. The critical coincidence of a search for new form with specific technical and economic developments has influenced architecture throughout the succeeding decades. These events may now hold interest for us because of their place in the history of American industrial buildings, because they instruct us about the origins of the modern vocabulary of architectural form, or because they cast light on the views of American cultural naivete held by European observers of American architecture.

6

[1] The theme of this article, the influence of American industrial buildings on the development of the visual vocabulary of modernism, was suggested by lectures given by Reyner Banham during the Columbia Summer Session 1982.

[2] For nineteenth century developments in American industrial architecture see William H. Pierson, Jr., *Industrial Architecture in the Berkshires*. (Ph.D. dissertation, Yale University, 1949.)

[3] Aly Ahmed Raafat, *Reinforced Concrete Construction in Architecture,* (New York, 1958).

[4] Robert B. Riley, "Grain Elevators: Symbols of Time, Place and Honest Building," *AIA Journal,* November 1977, 50-55.

[5] Translations from Gropius's article are from Tim and Charlotte Benton, *Architecture and Design: 1890-1939,* (New York, 1975).

[6] Le Corbusier's alteration of photographs is shown in Paul Turner, *The Education of Le Corbusier,* (Harvard Ph.D. dissertation published in 1977 by Garland Press, New York).

[7] Le Corbusier, *Toward a New Architecture,* (London, 1927), p. 33.

Pragmatism and Provinciality:
Italian Criticism of the American Plan
P.A. Morton

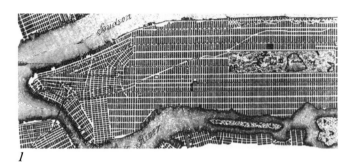

1

It is clear that the European in America never felt entirely fixed in place upon the continent. He had left the closed garden of the European landscape behind him, and his new natural environment was larger, more hostile, and above all, less bounded than any he had known before. The American was therefore the first European to experience the continuous flux of modern times, and his most characteristic literature, from Cooper and Melville to Whitman and Twain, celebrated images of homelessness, movement and continuous flow.[1]

The American, as a modern man, has felt the urge to plan his spaces and settlements in such a way as to root himself to the continent with as rigid structures as possible which nevertheless enable him to express his individuality freely. In this compulsion, the American reveals himself to be an existential being. "...at once a tiny atom in a vast sea of humanity and an individual who recognizes himself as being utterly alone."[2] The definition of the American as a European searching to make his home in a hostile world without bounding himself with European social and cultural systems continues to inform American planning sensibilities. Thus, in the New York City grid, the University of Virginia plan, the Illinois Institute of Technology, and American suburban developments, for example, the framework in which the parts are organized is immutable and rigidly laid down. Within this structure, the constituent elements can vary infinitely as long as they follow the formal system.

The largest scale example of this characteristic mode of planning is the New York City grid, laid out in 1811. The grid is transposed over New York's topography without deviations in response to local conditions such as hills or the shoreline. The buildings placed on the grid are wildly different in ornmentation, size, use and lot coverage, but they all obey the dictates of the grid. Leonardo Benevolo has likened the plan of New York City to the American Constitution. Just as the plan reduced "rules to

the minimum compatible with the technical necessities of community life, while making those few extremely rigid and unwavering" so the Constitution formulated the rules of political life "in such a way as to occasion minimal limitations to the citizens' private activities, being therefore reduced to a series of formal statements whose meaning was comprehensible only in relation to the application that is and has been made of them".[3]

Vincent Scully identifies this aspect of American planning with America's youth and the vast scale of her landscape. The potential for new social and political systems was paralleled in that for a new architecture. American architecture was the first modern architecture, in Scully's view, because of its responsiveness to what would become the universal conditions of modern life: continuity of space, lack of rootedness, "compulsion toward movement"[4], existentialism, pragmatism.

The University of Virginia is another example of this type of plan-making and can serve as the vehicle for further exploring this aspect of American architecture through the writings of three European critics: Manfredo Tafuri, Leonardo Benevolo and Aldo Rossi. The University was planned by Thomas Jefferson to be an example of proper building in America. He stated that "an University should not be a house but a village"[5]. His plan follows this ideal with a uniquely inventive distribution of the parts of the school. The central Rotunda, housing the library, classrooms and gymnasium, overlooks the Lawn, a space formed by two wings. These consist of small houses for each professor connected by students' rooms behind a colonnade. There are ten pavilions, each a different exercise in the use of classical architectural language. Behind the pavilions are gardens defined by the famous serpentine walls of one brick's thickness. Beyond the gardens, more student rooms and the dining rooms, collectively the "ranges", are placed.

The strictness of the plan and the simultaneous flexibility of the configurations of the pavilions is seen by Tafuri as an image of the attempted "reconciliation of the mobility of values with the stability of principles, the individual impulse—always stimulated to the point of anarchy—with the social dimension"[6] by American intellectuals. This "unresolved contradiction" is symptomatic of the American tendency to reduce architecture to the level of interchangeable parts within a rigidly structured context, as well as characteristic of the conflict between the restraint demanded by democracy and the freedoms it promises. The "nostalgic evocation of European values" was

2. University of Virginia, drawing attributed to Thomas Jefferson and Cornelia Randolph

ironic in a country whose "drive to economic and industrial development was leading to the concrete and intentional destruction of these values."[7]

Tafuri's critique is acute in that it identifies the perpetual conflict between the needs of the community and the demands of the individual in democratic systems. This is reflected in the "ambiguous conscience of American intellectuals" who pay lip service to democratic principles while espousing cultural models that evolved under monarchies and other feudal systems. Tafuri's particular polemical viewpoint makes him unable to analyze this attitude as anything but regressive utopianism seeking to avoid the logical progression of capitalism's development.

Benevolo, on the other hand, has a similar ideological bias, but regards the University of Virginia in a more benign manner. He points out that this and contemporary structures were the reflection of an attitude that

> reveals a serenity, a detachment from the ferocious European battle—exactly the quality that appeared in Jefferson's architecture as breadth, freedom, spontaneity—which hinted at the possibilities of a new development, less subtle but freer and more open.[8]

He prefaces this reluctant praise with the statement that it would have been easy for Europeans of the time to conclude that Jefferson and the Americans understood nothing of the cultural significance of the forms or methods they adopted.[9] This results from the fact that Americans "took to America only what they regarded as useful, with a sense of moderation which is, in a sense, the real core of their national tradition".[10] This "limitation in cultural relations" caused America's architectural independence from Europe, according to Benevolo.

Aldo Rossi does not regard this pragmatic, selective use of European building precedents as a "limitation". Rather, he sees parallels between the American city and his own work in its use of established types.

> The market in Providence, towns in Nantucket... seaports like Galveston— all seem to be, and are, constructed of preexisting elements that are then deformed by their own context... Perhaps no urban construct in the world equals that of a city like New York. New York is a city of monuments such as I did not believe could exist.[11]

Rossi's own work is based on his concept of analogy which is expressed in a design process involving preexisting elements which are formally defined, but the meaning of which evolves only with the process. The concept of type is central to this process since it defines those preexisting elements. The city "presents itself through certain clearly

2

defined elements such as house, school, church, factory, monument".[12] As with Benevolo's comparison between the New York City grid and the United States Constitution, these parts have meaning only in the context of their application. For Rossi, the University of Virginia is "strikingly" like his work because of its use of the Pantheon, the colonnade, etc. to create "unexpected meaning" in its totality.

The American use of pattern books, the tendency to use forms whole in new contexts and the specificity of American planning solutions are virtues, in Rossi's eyes, which go "beyond any utopian or formalistic vision of the city".[13] Rather than degenerate, provincial manifestations of cultural poverty, American cities and architecture are examples of Rossi's *city of parts* in which it is the dynamic created between the autonomous pieces of the city which gives it character. By defining the city in this way, there is greater freedom of choice in the city's makeup, one of the primary objectives of American planning.

[1]Scully, Vincent, *Modern Architecture,* New York, 1961, p. 17.
[2]Scully, *op. cit.,* p. 10.
[3]Benevolo, Leonardo, *History of Modern Architecture,* Cambridge, Mass., 1977, p. 212.
[4]Scully, *op. cit.,* p. 27.
[5]Guinness, Desmond and Julius Trousdale Sadler Jr., *Mr. Jefferson Architect,* New York, 1973, p. 120.
[6]Tafuri, Manfredo, *Architecture and Utopia,* Cambridge, Mass., 1976, p. 30.
[7]Tafuri, *op. cit.,* p. 34.
[8]Benevolo, op. cit., p. 206.
[9]*Ibid.*
[10]*Ibid.*
[11]Rossi, Aldo, *The Architecture of the City,* Cambridge, Mass., 1982, p. 15.
[12]Rossi, *op. cit.,* p. 18.
[13]*Ibid.*

Design and the Public Good
Richard Plunz

This material appears courtesy of the MIT Press. It is excerpted from the introduction to Design and the Public Good: Selected Writings, 1930-1980, by Serge Chermayeff, *edited by Richard Plunz, MIT Press, 1982.*

Serge Chermayeff occupies a unique position in the evolution of twentieth-century architecture. His legacy is complex, and time will serve to reinforce his importance. His contribution is a composite of several periods and pre-occupations, each with its own consciousness. Included must be his role in British design innovation in the thirties, extended in a limited but significant way later in the United States. Also included must be his initiatives in design education and research in the United States: his curriculum of a Department of Design at Brooklyn College; his further pedagogical development of the Lazlo Moholy-Nagy curriculum at the Institute of Design in Chicago; and finally, his extended involvement with teaching and research at Harvard and Yale. Also included must be Chermayeff's position as critic, in the most profound sense, involving both architectural and social commentary that reached beyond popular journalism. Above all, he has been an architect, but an architect who is also a literary person.

The political dimension of Chermayeff's thinking must be placed within the tradition of reform socialism in England dating back to the late nineteenth century, most specifically within the realm of the Fabian Society and Labor Party. Both organizations were concerned with pragmatic goals of immediate political reform rather than with struggles to achieve utopia. Both focused more on the inequities of capitalism than on promoting a holistic new vision. They were not revolutionary. . . . The English modernism of the thirties cannot be separated from the left political ideals that nurtured it.

The public forum was an extensive one. From the beginning, Chermayeff's input was literary. It was also good theatre, with Chermayeff playing the "brilliant talker and wit, not too austere in his conceptions of the artist's role," as he has been described by Noel Carrington.[1] His visibility to the public led to difficulties with the political right, however.

Ultimately, the war led to Chermayeff's removal to the United States. After immigration, he extended his involvement with ARP ("Air Raid Precaution"), publishing a series of articles and otherwise attempting to promote discussion. In general, he transferred his political sensibilities from the British to American context, connecting with the network of progressive architects and organizations that had been fostered by the Depression years or that had originated with the crisis of war. In San Francisco he supported the formation of "Telesis,"[2] and in New York the Federation of Architects, Engineers, Chemists, and Technicians (FAECT), the most powerful of the several

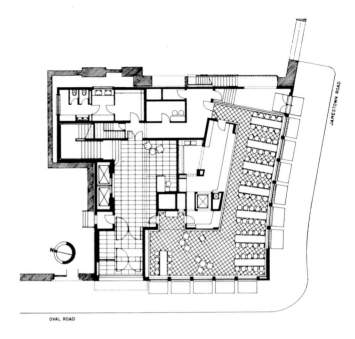

1

labor unions for architects and draftsmen.[3] He participated in forming the American chapter of the International Congress for Modern Architecture (CIAM), the American Society of Planners and Architects (ASPA),[4] and the Architects Committee of the National Council of Soviet-American Friendship.[5] . . .

The dilemmas presented to architects as the McCarthy era unfolded are an important, if neglected, segment of the history of the profession. For liberal architects within a profession that represents a quite fragile public art subservient to the sources of economic and political power, the period forced difficult choices. As Victor Navasky relates, there was ample evidence "of how deep were the divisions that beset the liberal community in the third great cold war conflict—the war between those who thought of themselves as progressives and those who inhabited what they like to call the vital center."[6] Consistent with tradition, the compromises of the "vital center" were paramount to commercial survival for architects, leaving the progressives adrift.

For Chermayeff's circle, difficulties did arise. For example, the Architect's Committee of the National Council of Soviet-American Friendship, which was active between

2. *View of Gilbey Hall*
3. *Entertainment Hall, Bexhill,*
   Sussex, 1934

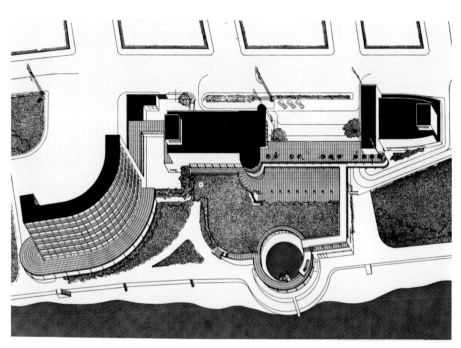

2

3

1944 and 1946, found itself listed by the U.S. attorney general as a subversive organization in 1952. Those on the leadership roster, almost entirely AIA members, were thus prevented from gaining approval for certain government work. Ultimately some of the membership renounced their affiliation with the National Council in order to obtain clearance for work.[7]

By the close of the forties, even the politically ecumenical American Society of Planners and Architects (ASPA) had long since disappeared. Between 1944 and 1946 it had pursued a wide range of concerns in relation to urban problems and modern architecture. Its almost eighty members included a cross section of architects who would mold the direction of United States architecture in the next two decades: Chermayeff, Louis Kahn, Marcel Breuer, Walter Gropius, Jose Luis Sert, Siegfried Giedion, Henry Russell-Hitchcock, Gordon Bunshaft, John Johansen, Philip Johnson, I. M. Pei, Eero Saarinen, Hugh Stubbins, and other newly trained Americans waiting to launch their careers.

It was against the backdrop of professional ambiguities toward social commitments that, in 1954, Chermayeff finally resigned from the AIA, which was all that remained

of the professional organizations of the previous decade. ... Chermayeff's censure of the mainstream architectural profession in the United States is consistent with a critical position that found its origins in England, but, by comparison, the American context for architectural practice in the fifties would only serve to heighten that critique. ...

At the outset, the United States held out the promise of renewed practice, especially in California, which attracted Chermayeff as it had Schindler or Neutra. In spite of war, he received commissions in California in quick succession—the Mayhew House and then Horn House—but by this time the desire to practice was no longer paramount. Work did not come easily, and commercial practice in postwar America would obviously entail the kind of compromise of intellectual involvement that bordered on dereliction.[8] Chermayeff demurred. Design activity became, like his painting, a pleasurable activity rather than a livelihood.

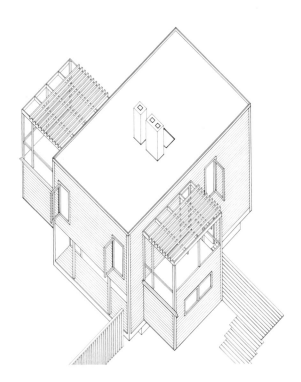

4

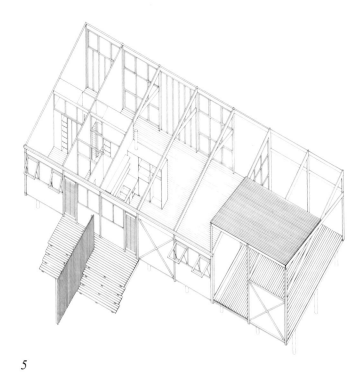

5

In his youth Chermayeff was preoccupied with the most populist aspects of twenties modernity: jazz, dance, and digression into surrealist painting. Ballroom dancing was a serious activity for several years, reflecting his fascination with the great American bands and his penchant for performance in the milieu of the Barclay or Savoy. Lacking a formal education in architecture, he is not a product of nineteenth-century eclectic academicism or its antidote in Teutonic functionalism. He is, instead, a product of twentieth-century eclecticism—an original, and eccentric in the best sense. His initation into architecture was gradual, with his early formation aligned as much with the *deco moderne* of the 1925 Paris Exhibition as with anything else. ... It was a gregarious period, which imparted to his later design an openness to embellishment—almost flamboyance, in contrast to the work of many others in Britain.

If there is a common purpose that links all of Chermayeff's design, it must be innovation in program and in the application of new technology. This "design without precedent" rendered style without precedent. He exploited a myriad of "new materials and new methods" to their fullest in terms of impact on both program and aesthetic. ...

In subsequent years, as Chermayeff obtained commissions, his collaboration with the German emigre engineer Felix Sammuely was extremely effective in furthering technological innovation. This collaboration included the Entertainment Hall at Bexhill, Gilbey House, the laboratories for the Imperial Chemical Industries, and Bentley Wood. In Berlin, Sammuely had produced the first welded steel-frame building, and he set the same precedent for Mendelsohn and Chermayeff at Bexhill.

Bentley Wood, while reverting to more traditional materials, also represented significant technological innovation. For example, the timber structural grid, designed for spatial flexibility, was constructed in a manner not dissimilar to steel. Prefabricated timber sections were assembled on the site using special connectors at the joints that could be tightened over the life of the building to compensate for shrinkage.

In general, Chermayeff's design has exhibited a devoted willingness to experiment, without undue compulsion for aesthetic strictures. ... His experimentation with wood continued in the United States, especially in the series of structures built on Cape Cod in the early fifties

6. Chermayeff House, New Haven, Connecticut, 1963

6

that were constructed of standard timber framing adapted to new structural forms incorporating new materials, principally "Homosote." Of course, in microcosm much of Chermayeff's prodigious production of furnishings and product designs evidences concerns kindred to those of his buildings: the numerous chairs [9]—for example, the Plan Armchair W-5, with its removable upholstery, or the early experiments with plastics—the radio cabinets for E. K. Cole, Ltd.; or the pianos that slightly adjusted the traditional idiom. Much later, in a totally different context, the new technology of the computer was embraced as a design tool in *Community and Privacy* and indirectly contributed to the design for his own house on Lincoln Street in New Haven, in many ways his most remarkable house.

History will reveal misconceptions, complexities, and ironies about Chermayeff's life and career. For example, Leonardo Benevolo's implication that Chermayeff's contribution to the Mendelsohn partnership could be discounted is without basis.[10] One has only to reflect on the mastery of the auditorium at Bexhill, which was Chermayeff's execution. Ironically, Bentley Wood, one of the most accomplished buildings of the decade of "social revolution" in Britain, was identified much later by John Summerson as "the most aristocratic building of the decade."[11] It probably was. Certainly it is a minor masterpiece and is in its own right very much a sequel (if unintentional) to the legacy of Lutyens. Chermayeff's buildings have a significance far beyond their small number. The Gilbey House has captured renewed interest today. Hugh Casson praised it at the time of its completion as "sound vernacular design—a city building [that] is primarily an element of the street"[12] It was nonmonumental urban infill, which responded through a new language to the nineteenth-century urbanism of its surroundings—"contextualism" with base, middle, and top, the latter cornice composed of covered terrace and repetitive skylights. Three decades later, Chermayeff described Venturi's winning entry to the Yale Mathematics Building competition

as déjà vu,[13] and it was, considering the similarities (if unintentional) to Gilbey House. The ironies of the century and its architectural elaboration will be many, and for all sides.

[1]Noel Carrington, *Industrial Design in Britain,* London, 1976, p. 139.

[2]"Telesis: The Birth of a Group," *Pencil Points* XXIII, July 1942, pp. 27-28.

[3]"Activities," *Task* V, Spring 1944, p. 36.

[4]Miscellaneous material on the American Chapter of the International Congress for Modern Architecture (CIAM) and on the American Society of Planners and Architects (ASPA) may be found with the Chermayeff Archive of Papers from the American Society of Planners and Architects, Widener Library, Harvard University.

[5]See "National Council of Soviet-American Friendship" and "Committee of the Arts, Sciences and Professions," Serge Chermayeff Archive, Avery Library, Columbia University.

[6]Victor S. Navasky, *Naming Names,* New York, 1980, p. 47.

[7]Memorandum from Vernon DeMars dated March 31, 1952, under "National Council of Soviet-American Friendship," Serge Chermayeff Archive, Avery Library, Columbia University.

[8]Chermayeff's ire in relation to the AIA increased when Ralph Walker became president in 1949. See "The Profession of Architecture," a talk given at the Institute of Design, Chicago, dated November 2, 1950. Serge Chermayeff Archive, Avery Library, Columbia University.

[9]Some of Chermayeff's furnishings, especially chairs, were adapted from production on the Continent and are therefore of complex attribution. Some research has been initiated on this general problem. See Dennis Sharp, Tim Benton and Barbie Campbell Cole, *Pel and Tubular Furniture of the Thirties,* London, 1977.

[10]Leonardo Benevolo, *History of Modern Architecture,* 2 vols., Cambridge, Mass., 1971, p. 588.

[11]John Summerson, "Introduction," in Trevor Dannatt, *Modern Architecture in Britain,* London, 1959, p. 17.

[12]Hugh Casson, "Good Building and Bad Theater," *Night and Day,* September 9, 1937, p. 2.

[13]See Ellen Perry Berkeley, "Mathematics at Yale," *Architectural Forum* CXXXIII, July/August 1970, pp. 63-65; "Mathematics at Yale: Readers Respond," *Architectural Forum* CXXXII, October 1970, pp. 64-66.

The Contextualism of Eliel Saarinen
Carolyn Senft

1

2

3

Eliel Saarinen was one of the first major European architects of the twentieth century to immigrate to the United States. While still residing in Finland, Saarinen had taken extended annual trips to various parts of Europe to see architectural work, particularly that which exemplified ideas sympathetic with his own theories. The publications which made their way into Finland did not sufficiently describe current architectural endeavors. In 1907, for example, Saarinen's trip included interviews with contemporaries Joseph Olbrich and Peter Behrens in Germany. For similar reasons, Saarinen chose to make an extended visit to the United States in 1923 which led to his immigration. The trip was also motivated by the hope for greater opportunities to obtain large scale commissions which were no longer plentiful in Finland or the rest of Europe.

Certain issues arose for Saarinen by coming to America to continue his career. The theories which were nurtured during more than two decades of architectural practice in Finland might not remain valid in a new cultural, social and economic context.

Additionally, Saarinen's second place award in the Chicago Tribune Tower Competition in 1922 cannot be overlooked. This event was primarily responsible for bringing the Finnish architect to the attention of his contemporaries in the United States. The esteem Americans held for the proposal became exaggerated because it was submitted by a European. Louis Sullivan, one of the jurors of the competition, expressed surprise "that a 'foreigner' should possess the insight required to penetrate to the depths of the sound, strong, kindly and aspiring idealism which lies at the core of the American people".[1] Consequently, in order to understand the position Saarinen attained in early twentieth century American architecture, it is necessary to investigate the development of Saarinen's ideas, both as a product of his native environment and as they were influenced by the events and work of individual architects in the States.

Saarinen's work shows the influence of various other architects. As he stated, "One does not live in a vacuum; the work of others affect the efforts of any creative mind".[2] What

he tried to avoid was becoming infatuated with a style and attempting to apply it to his projects regardless of their function, context, materials or method of construction. Above all, Saarinen was concerned with attaining what he regarded as truthfulness in his designs.

> My colleagues and I, in Finland, adhered to the theory that function and material decide the nature of form. This was by no means an original thought; rather, it was a fundamental one. But because this fundamental thought had for so long been buried beneath all kinds of accumulated stylistic nonsense, it was necessary to dig it out from its ornamental grave and to reinstate it in its place of honesty.[3]

Saarinen found that some of his American colleagues shared his views, notably Louis Sullivan. For example, at the World's Columbian Exposition in Chicago in 1893, Sullivan's Transportation Building stood in contrast to the other buildings which were Classical in style and whitewashed to emulate marble. This building

> gloried in the fact that it . . . was

4. *Hvittrask: Elevation.*
5. *Hvittrask: Site plan.*
6. *Gesellius and Saarinen:*
   Molchow-Haus, Mark Branden-
   burg, Germany, 1905-7. View.
7. *Molchow-Haus: Plan.*

4

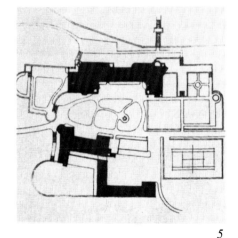

5

6

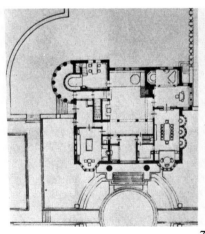

7

stucco and not marble, that it was only a shed the purpose of which was to furnish cover for an exhibition of locomotives and Pullman cars.[4]

Two early buildings by Saarinen, designed with his partners Herman Gesellius and Armas Lindgren, are particularly concerned with materials. In both the Pohjola Insurance Company Building (1899-1901) and the architect's residence and studio at Hvittrask (1902) stone is the prominent material, soapstone in the former case and granite in the latter.

The use of stone, especially granite, had acquired symbolic significance for Finnish architects in the late nineteenth century. It was appreciated for being hard to work, which served as a metaphor for "...a strong national foundation for Finland...".[5] Consequently, it seemed an appropriate material for a country searching for its own style.[6]

The stone in both cases is used in its natural rough-cut state. These architects' concern for the honest expression of materials was akin to that of Henry Hobson Richardson whose

work served as a model for their own. The Pohjola Insurance Company Building (*1*) bears close resemblance to Richardson's Cheney Block (*2*) in the articulation of its architectural elements. In the architects's residence at Hvittrask, (*3,4* and *5*) the stone is used in conjunction with wood and red tiles. The granite contributes to creating a romantic, informal design, which Saarinen considered appropriate for the gently sloping, densely wooded site.

Several years later, practicing with Gesellius, Saarinen designed the

8. *Saarinen: Chicago Tribune
Tower Competition entry, 1922.
Perspective.*
9. *Gesellius, Lingren and Saarinen:
Railroad station, Helsinki,
1905-14. View.*

8

9

Molchow-Haus in Germany. (*6* and *7*)
In contrast to the highly-textured surfaces of the residence in Hvittrask,
stucco is the dominant material. Its
crisp simplicity reinforces a design
which is formal in character,
Saarinen's response to a flat, open
site.

The Chicago Tribune Tower
Competition (*8*) presented Saarinen
with two new opportunities. Not only
did he have to confront the "intricate
problem of the lofty steel-framed
structure"[9], but also whether and
how to express the American character in the building's delineation. His
design emphasizes vertical movement
and "diverts the eye... by its easy upward sweep".[10] In the Helsinki Railroad Station of two decades earlier,
Saarinen had also expressed verticality by articulating the corners with
uninterrupted upward elements. (*9*)
On the Tribune tower, Saarinen used
various elements to continue the
movement skyward. This is emphasized by statues at the top of each setback which, rather than terminating
one's line of vision, direct one's vision upward to the next setback. The
proposal gave the impression to
Saarinen's contemporaries of having
the same potential for unlimited
height that steel construction was
then considered to have. This proposal also evoked the "aspiring
idealism"[11] of Americans in the early
twentieth century about which Sullivan had spoken.

Saarinen's first built commission
in the United States, Cranbrook
Academy, is a strong contrast to the
singular form of the Tribune Tower.
(*10* and *11*) Each articulated element
of the complex is expressive of its particular function, yet they create a
cohesive entity. Unlike the symmetry

of a Beaux-Arts plan, long associated with educational complexes,
Saarinen's design for the academy
does not consist of similarly designed
buildings on either side of major or
minor axes. The informality of the
design was a response to the school's
rural setting. Saarinen's personal yet
restrained style of ornament articulates the buildings' elements; pediments, pergolas and doorways are
emphasized to reinforce the complex's
unity at a larger scale.

Saarinen's work shows him to
have been a true contextualist. He recognized that each project had to be
approached on its own terms since the
factors which affect the built form,
function, materials, construction
method and site, change from one
project to the next. He believed that
honestly expressing the nature of
these factors would create buildings
appropriate for their time and place.

> Architecture embraces the whole
> form-world of man's physical
> accommodations, from the intimacy of his room to the comprehensive labyrinth of the large
> metropolis. Within this broad
> field of creative activities, the
> architect's ambition must be to
> develop a form language expressing the *best* aims of *his
> time*—and of no other time—and
> to cement the various features of
> his expressive forms into a good
> interrelation, and ultimately into
> the rhythmic coherence of the
> multi-formed organism of the
> city.[10]

Saarinen's proposal for the
Chicago Tribune tower exemplified
the nature of his design method in his
use of ornament, specifically, the
statues, to reinforce the design concept at all scales. In his work, he
demonstrated to architects in Europe
and America that ornament need not

10. *Saarinen: Cranbrook School for Boys and Girls, Bloomfield Hills, Michigan, 1924. Bird's eye perspective.*
11. *Cranbrook: View.*

be arbitrarily applied. Saarinen participated in the international creation of a design theory informing architecture which is both functional and responsive to its context.

[1]Christ-Janer, Albert, *Eliel Saarinen*, Chicago, 1979, p. 58.
[2]Creese, Walter L., "Saarinen's Tribune Design", *Journal of the Society of Architectural Historians,* vol. 6, n. 3-4, p. 1.
[3]Christ-Janer, p. 12
[4]Tallmadge, Thomas E., *The Story of Architecture in America*, New York, 1936, p. 210.
[5]Tuomi, Ritva, "On the Search for a National Style", *Abacus* (Yearbook of the Museum of Finnish Architecture), 1979, p. 86.
[6]For several centuries, Finland was ruled by Sweden. Its culture was, therefore, significantly influenced by that of Sweden. By the late nineteenth century, the Finns, then under Russian rule, began to seek independence. This movement was reflected in the search for a Finnish architectural style.
[7]Christ-Janer, p. 58.
[8]Creese, p. 3.
[9]Christ-Janer, p. 58.
[10]Christ-Janer, p. xvii.

10

11

Foundations: American House Types
Steven Holl

This article is excerpted from *Pamphlet Architecture #9:* "Rural and Urban House Types in North America."

The birth of a 'type' is dependent on the existence of a series of buildings having between them an obvious formal and functional analogy. In other words, when a 'type' is determined in the practice or theory of architecture, it already has an existence as an answer to a complex of ideologic religious or practical demands which arise in a given historical condition of whatever culture.

. . . the formative process of a typology is not just a classifying or statistical process but one carried out for definite formal ends. Typological series do not arise only in relation to the physical functions of buildings but are tied to the configuration. The fundamental 'type' of the circular shrine, for example, is independent of the functions, sometimes complex, which such buildings must fulfil.

From "On the Typology of Architecture" by Guilio Carlo Argan, translated by Joseph Rykwert.

In even a cursory study of American house types, it is important to focus on basic forms in order to understand more complex and sophisticated forms. Just as rhythm and melody are considered basic to the study of music, so the elemental interrelation of plan and section in building type is fundamental to the study of architecture. If syncopation and triadic harmony should be suspended from an elementary music lesson, so complicated variations in style should be suspended from an elementary architectural analysis. In comparing and studying American vernacular architecture, American

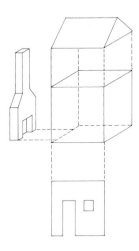

Rural: One Room House
The nearly cubic form of the basic one room house is constant whether it is of clapboard in New England, of stone in Utah, of brick in Virginia or of sod in Nebraska.

folklorists, historians and geographers have, for several decades, used the tool of typological classification. This method, analyzing and organizing buildings according to type, has recently reemerged as an analytical tool in current architectural theory.

In numerous papers and field research, historian Fred Kniffen has stressed the distinctions in methods of study of American houses. According to Kniffen, the typical architectural historian's interest is "in superficial treatment that may disguise a single, old and fundamental form as generally Georgian, Federal, Greek Revival or Gothic."[1] Professor Kniffen carried forward a typological approach in studying American vernacular architecture. Beginning in the 1930's with unchronicled rural American house forms, he observed and presented recurring typological continui-

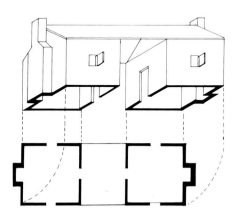

Rural: Dog Trot House
The dog trot house consists of two equal one-story rooms on either side of a central hall, joined by a common roof. In the South and Southwest the passage functioned as a shady breezeway.

ties. Preferring the cultural uniformity of the rural dwelling, Kniffen wrote, "There are, architecturally speaking, two cultures, rural and urban."[2]

From a different perspective, similar conclusions were reached by Edna Scofield in her 1936 article on Tennessee house types when she wrote,

A purely natural landscape is one which has never been occupied by man. An area which is unified upon the basis of the way in which man has used and transformed the natural landscape is a cultural landscape.[3]

Scofield attempted to define house types within a cultural geography comparable to a classification of species in the natural sciences. Citing the simple one room house as the seed from which nearly all houses

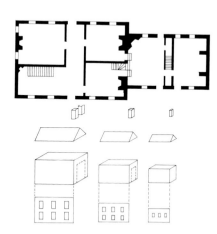

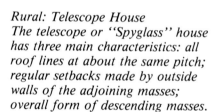

Rural: Telescope House
The telescope or "Spyglass" house has three main characteristics: all roof lines at about the same pitch; regular setbacks made by outside walls of the adjoining masses; overall form of descending masses.

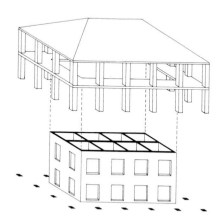

Rural: Plantation House
The plantation type is common in the Southeast, especially Louisiana, but examples have been built as far away as South Dakota. The galleries are not applied, but are recessed from the geometric whole.

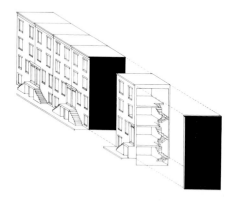

Urban: Father-Son-Holy Ghost
This type, also known as the band-box, developed in Philadelphia with lot sizes of 13 × 20 feet. The type, dating from c. 1750, consists of one room on each of three or four floors.

have sprung, she wrote, "The original one room house represents the origin of a given species, for there are species of houses, and also different varieties of a given species."[4]

Typology, in the work of these cultural historians, was arrived at in an a posteriori way, from observation of recurring indigenous house types. This method is distinct from the academic propositions of architectural classification originating in the work of Jean-Nicolas-Louis Durand (1760-1834). Durand's inductively defined building "genres" were the result of an a priori derivation and were meant to serve as models. As a further development, the nineteenth century interest in typology centered on the belief in a universal theory of architecture which would apply to all buildings, in all places, at all times.

The houses presented here are not meant to serve as models. This investigation seeks to illuminate fundamental patterns in the interrelationship of culture and architecture. To do so, the house types have been divided into rural and urban groups. Whereas urban types develop out of the contiguous interlocking of houses within city blocks, rural types evolve from the relationship of the house to the earth and sky. The house is an isolated event revealed in an unspoiled perspective of hills and trees.

Within a collection of various rural house types, common characteristics are found:

1) recurring plan/section schemata, regardless of stylistic treatment;

2) adherence to geometric simplicity in everything from overall mass to elements such as porches,

windows and doors;

3) proportions such that detail is rendered subordinate to mass;

4) ornamentation which is developed from craft, methods of construction and the nature of materials.

Within a collection of urban house types the common principles are:

1) definition of a public street or place;

2) three types of walls: public street facades, party or blind walls, and walls internal to the block or courtyard;

3) relation to an overall city plan or morphology.

In both the rural and urban types, a spirit of geometry, a sense of independent thought, a consistent measure and proportion of detail and an overall coherence are principal characteristics.

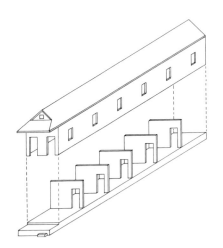

Urban: Shotgun House
The large, square blocks of the New Orleans city layout and the narrow lot divisions conditioned the development of a house in which one room aligned with the next.

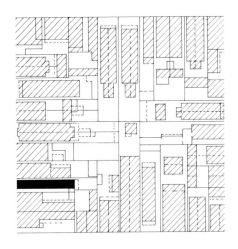

Plan: Typical New Orleans block Several double shotguns with a single shotgun shown in black.

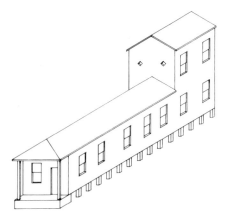

Urban: Camel Back Shotgun House This variation includes a second story addition at the rear of the house. Because of its one story alignment with the street front, the camel back was taxed as a single story building.

Geometric simplicity is a persistent and unwavering characteristic; with two doors, two windows and a fireplace, the one room house is a picture of geometric clarity, its cubic form crisply cut into a steep triangular gable of the roof. Simplicity of form is reinforced by the location of windows and doors. They are subordinated to the mass, being cut directly into it without elaboration around the openings. Even in the complex plantation house, the geometric mass of the house is never violated. The porch is not an added element, but part of an overall, nearly transparent whole which retains geometric absoluteness.

In some cases, symmetry orders the location of windows, but in many types a dissonant rhythm emerges. The random window openings of the American rural house appeared to

Thoreau "as if each occupant had punched a hole where his necessities required." Windows and doors freely arranged on a surface without alignment and symmetry emphasize the wall rather than the subdivisions within it.

In American house types, geometric rigor is chosen over complicated programmatic forces again and again. Attention to simple elements and a non-theoretical sense of proportion underlie the strength of these works.

In describing how the carpenter-architect sacrificed certain physical needs to achieve geometric clarity, Henry Glassie wrote:

The house is an expression of a cultural idea that valued the intellectual model over emotional need. It is not that the spaces provided by the house for hu-

man action were dysfunctional, but that the people were willing to endure chilly corners or rooms that may have felt a bit spacious or cramped in order to live in a house that was a perfect representation of an idea.[5]

In writing about the precedence given to the square form, Glassie goes on:

The squared volume was probably comfortably familiar, foremost to meet the needs of personal space; clearly his major directive was used to adhere to an intellectual model that demanded a specific geometric image.[6]

The compositional clarity and formal simplicity of vernacular houses comprised an important formal answer to spiritual and physical needs.

In these houses, detail is always subordinated to the overall form. Whether we are speaking of the glazed

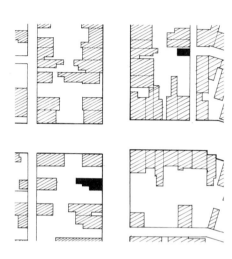

Plan: St. Louis, Missouri
Geyer Avenue and Rear Geyer
Avenue, with flounder houses.

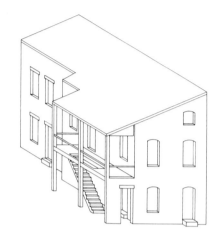

Urban: Flounder House
An urban house form called
"flounder," "half house" or "half
flounder" appears to be an acciden-
tal form but is actually a deliberate
one, with numerous examples in old
St. Louis and Alexandria, Virginia.

the merely fashionable. The symbolic power of these buildings stands as a silent argument to those champions of the academic who reject vernacular constructions as without text and theory and therefore irrational and meaningless. As a cultural expression, these houses are part of an elemental stock of forms in which coherence and emotional feeling can be detected; they exhibit theory in the same sense that Cassirer referred to when he wrote, "All intuition is bound up with theoretical thinking."

[1]Fred Kniffen, "Folk House: Key to Diffusion," *Annals of the Association of American Geographers,* 1965, pp. 549-577.
[2]*Ibid.*
[3]Edna Scofield, "The Evolution and Development of Tennessee Houses," *Journal of the Tennessee Academy of Science,* volume II, 1936.
[4]*Ibid.*
[5]Henry Glassie, *Folk Housing in Middle Virginia: Structural Analysis of Historical Artifacts,* Knoxville, 1973.
[6]*Ibid.*

brick which forms a "black diapering" pattern on the wall of a telescope house, or of the cypress detail work on the handrail of a plantation house, the relation of detail to mass is consistent. Only in our own decade does this principle seem completely out of balance. We have, at one extreme, the absence of detail in unresolved constructions and, at the other, assemblages with gross decorative elements, obliterating overall form.

In these houses, the whole is always greater than the sum of the parts. This architecture, at its most elemental, is mass, line and space organized through adherence to type and geometry. The elemental house is not made significant by decoration with representational symbols; it becomes representative in its totality. A representational facade applied to an amorphous entity will seldom be found.

In the case of contiguous urban houses, the facade is part of the definition of the street. Facade, blind walls and court or rear walls are unified by plan and section.

The characteristics manifested in these houses are the result of the carpenter-architect's uncompromising realization of an intuitively held goal. For us, such a goal must be held conceptually. A clear architectural idea, frankly stated, is analogous to the intuition which laid the path for the carpenter-architect. In today's circumstance, where numerous individuals work as a team to realize a construction, a unified result demands a clearly stated concept.

The carpenter-architects's adherence to type and geometry was an expression of values which transcend

Home in America: Early Alternatives to the Single-Family House
Graham S. Wyatt

This work owes a debt to the unpublished manuscript by Richard Plunz, Institutionalization of Housing Form in New York City, 1850-1950.

This work represents part of a larger research project funded by the American Institute of Architects and the Canada Mortgage and Housing Corporation. For their help I wish to thank Richard Plunz, Christine Boyer and Harry Toung.

The end of World War I represents a major economic watershed in the history of the United States. Although the war resulted in immense deficit financed consumption, it simultaneously stimulated the growth of fundamentally new industries. The automotive, petrochemical and electrical industries, no more than nascent before the war, entered the post-War era as potential corner-stones of American industry. Yet, America's "Return to Normalcy" was not an easy one. Millions of American servicemen returning from duty expected jobs while the new industries, no longer fat with war contracts, were forced to redirect their surplus productive capacity from guns to butter. The Federal government, realizing the political risks of high unemployment and the need for an economic growth rate which would support the newly-enlarged deficit, initiated a series of policies aimed at stimulating demand for American goods both at home and abroad.

One of the most fiscally successful policies on the home front was the encouragement of single-family home ownership among Americans. The inherent inefficiency of the single-family home made it a powerful economic stimulant. Each home required not only a serviced lot, foundations, walls and a roof but appliances, furnishings and ongoing maintenance. The owner of a single-family house probably needed a car, and cars required the construction of streets and highways. In addition to its economic benefits, the ownership of private property was felt to be politically and morally beneficial. In 1920 Frank Lowden, Governor of Illinois wrote:

> The security of a country depends in a large measure upon the number of homes owned by the dwellers therein. Family ties grow strongest in the house, however modest, which the family calls home. Love of home is at the root of love of country. We shall measure our progress in the years that lie ahead by the increase in the number of homes our people own.[1]

The Department of Labor became active in the promotion of home ownership by organizing "Own Your Home" shows acrosss the United States. The first New York show opened in June of 1919.[2] The Commerce Department, under Herbert Hoover, contributed to this effort by distributing planning and zoning information nationwide and by working to rationalize and standardize the American building industry.

Hoover's encouragement of suburbanization was supported by state and local legislation. During 1919 Alfred E. Smith, then governor of New York State, signed legislation allowing municipalities to exempt from taxation all residential buildings begun after April 1, 1919 and completed before April 1, 1922. New York City was among the five municipalities in the state which adopted tax exemption. The result was immediate; whereas the number of dwelling units in the city had decreased during 1918 and 1919, New York's outer boroughs experienced a housing boom between 1920 and 1927. The city government renewed tax exemption in 1922 and again in 1923, at which time changes were written into the law which favored the construction of one- and two-family houses over apartment buildings.[3]

If the spread of the single-family house seemed to suit the wishes of the government, it was not an idea that proved difficult to sell to the American public. Non-government affili-

1

ated organizations such as Better Homes in America, The Regional Planning Association of America and the Architects' Small House Service Bureau encouraged single-family housing with publicity which stressed efficiency, economy and scientific management in home design.[4]

Better Homes in America was founded in 1922 as a volunteer organization; by 1934 a total of 9000 volunteer committees represented Better Homes nationwide. Ray Lyman Wilbur, Better Homes in America President, summarized the organization's policy by writing:

> There is little question that our American life, if it is to proceed upward instead of downward, will move away from agglomerate living toward the small home unit.[5]

Other observers, less biased by potential financial benefit, made similar

1. 'Own Your Home' promotion
2. America's Little House, designed by Roger H. Bullard and Clifford C. Wendenack, Landscape by Annette Hoyt Flanders. The 'American Ideal', from hearth to garden, was justified in economic terms to the nearest cent.

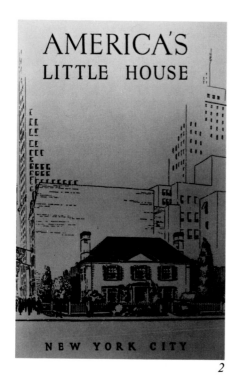

AMERICA'S LITTLE HOUSE

NEW YORK CITY

2

observations. In 1940, Catherine Bauer, member of the Regional Planning Association of America and co-organizer of the housing section of the Museum of Modern Art's 1932 International Style Exhibition, summarized forty years of changing American housing aspirations by writing:

> Today, most people with $10,000 income want compact, well planned homes. They would rather live on a quiet street near a country club than facing four lanes of traffic. ...[6]

The strategy adopted by the "Own Your Home" movement is exemplified by the construction of "America's Little House" on the corner of Park Avenue and 39th Street in 1934. This demonstration house was sponsored by Better Homes in America and the Columbia Broadcasting System. CBS built a radio

broadcast studio in what would have been the house's garage from which three national radio programs were broadcast each week. These broadcasts, in conjunction with a flood of publications, promoted the idea of single-family home ownership.

The House's English Georgian styling was selected to avoid the regional associations of Dutch, Colonial or Spanish, producing a house which "might be universally adapted throughout the United States."[7]

The architecture, furnishings and landscaping of America's Little House were selected with economy and efficiency in mind, yet these economies were suspiciously suggestive of the belt tightening which the prosperous American upper middle classes were undertaking in order to weather the Depression. America's Little House was to be a custom-built affair; it was not *housing for the masses.*

If the Little House represented the upper middle class ideal, the type underwent a series of transmutations that made it accessible to Americans of lower income. Most low-cost, single-family houses during this period were using conventional, on-site construction techniques. In New York City tax exemption, coupled with rapidly rising rents, made the proliferation of the single-family home virtually inevitable. During 1923, brick houses on tenth-of-an-acre sites in Queens typically sold for between $8,700 and $9,500 new. Frame houses of similar size and quality could be purchased for between $6,700 and $8,700, and in Brooklyn, five-room frame houses were priced as low as $5,000 apiece.[8] Tax exemption meant that money which would otherwise have been used to pay property taxes could pay off a second mortgage.

Payment of the first mortgage, including amortization was equal to what a homeowner had previously been paying in rent (or was often a little less). Louis Gold, a New York builder, summarized the situation in testimony before the New York State Commission of Housing and Regional Planning in 1924:

> Prior to exemption ... people would not buy houses. They were afraid to buy. The rents in apartment houses now are compelling people to buy these (single-family) houses. They save a great deal by owning them.[9]

In spite of industrial production techniques, economies of scale and tax exemption, the least expensive of these freestanding houses was still priced beyond the means of the majority of the untapped housing market. Even during the boom year of 1926, sixty percent of all American families still earned less than $2,500 per year (i.e., they could afford $45 to $50 per month in rent). First mortgage payments of $45 through $50 were just sufficient to purchase a $5,000 home. In other words, sixty percent of the nation's population was in an income bracket which would not enable it to purchase even the cheapest developer house in the suburbs of New York.

Acknowledging this fact, New York State legislation passed in 1922 allowed life insurance companies, for the first time, to invest ten percent of their assets in the erection of apartment houses provided the rent to be charged did not exceed $9.00 per room (i.e., $45.00 for a five room apartment).[10]

The $9.00 per room limit proved extremely difficult to achieve with conventional apartment house construction, but a viable alternative had been proposed three years earlier by

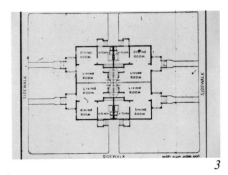

3

5

4

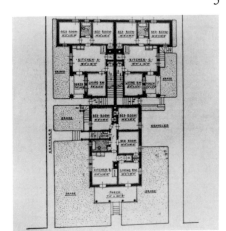

6

3. *Plan, Party Wall Housing Project, Harry Allen Jacobs, 1919*
4. *View of Party Wall Housing Project*
5. *West 239th Street Housing, Bronx, New York, Clarence Stein, 1919*
6. *Plan, West 239th Street Housing*

New York architect Harry Allen Jacobs. Jacobs sought to combine the benefits of free-standing houses with the economies of multiple-family dwellings. In a proposal submitted to the Mayor's Commission on Housing of 1919, Jacobs called for the building of six-room houses in groups of four. Each two-story home had both front and side entrances, a double exposure and a private garden. The design allowed considerable savings in construction cost over a single-family home offering similar amenities. Shared party-walls reduced the expense of exterior wall, foundations and roofing. Water, electrical, gas, telephone and sewer service could be shared among units and construction management costs would be reduced.[11]

By placing each home in the corner of its lot, a density of sixteen homes per acre could be achieved, as compared with eleven units per acre which was standard at the time. Jacob's house also saved money for the home owner: reduced exterior wall cut down on both maintenance and on heat loss. The corner lot location of the house left a garden which, Jacobs argued, was more private and more easily maintained than the garden surrounding a detached home.

The proof of Jacob's argument lay in his cost analysis: Jacob's houses could be sold at $4,000 each leaving an estimated profit of $1,450 per home for the developer. Alternately, each home could be rented at a profit for $40 per month ($6.70 per room).

Although Jacob's houses are rather prosaic in their architectural expression, they represent an interesting union of two distinctly different housing types, retaining many of the advantages of both. Jacob's housing development has the appearance of a neighborhood of generously spaced suburban houses; each house presents its narrow face to the street, a reversal of the current British and European practice in which grouped houses were typically aligned parallel to the street, expressing the grouping of units at the expense of the home-like quality of the whole.

Also during 1919, Clarence S. Stein erected a low-density, low-cost housing project on West 239th Street in the Bronx. Stein's scheme grouped six single-family units within a building. Like the Jacobs design, Stein oriented his buildings with their narrow, house-like "fronts" to the street, creating a streetscape of widely spaced houses with balconies, front porches and generous front yards. Each unit has a private street-level entrance but has the disadvantages that ground floor units have bedrooms located directly adjacent to the play yard and that second floor units are entered through an uncomfortably small vestibule at the bottom of a flight of stairs.

The significance of Stein's scheme lies in its site plan. By taking advantage of a 250 foot deep block, he orients the buildings with their long dimension perpendicular to the street. Stein manages to equal or exceed the density of contemporary German Siedlungen or British Council Housing.[12] At the same time he creates a streetscape which suggests well-spaced, single-family houses and is demonstrably American in its appearance. The interior of the block contains alternating formal gardens and playgrounds while on the exterior of the block each house is set back from the street by a front yard and separated from its neighbors by usable side yards.

The novelty of both Jacob's and Stein's designs becomes clearer when they are compared with German or British grouped housing of this period or with American designs which followed the European pattern. Among American designs, Stein's first Sunnyside Gardens housing is both the most successful and most famous of this type. This project is widely known today, not simply because it was built (most of Stein's 239th Street project was not) but because it soon came to be seen as an early American expression of European Modernist principles.

7. *Block Plan, West 239th Street Housing*
8. *Interior Courtyard, Sunnyside Gardens, Queens, New York, Clarence Stein and Henry Wright, 1924*
9. *Site Plan, Archibald Bull Housing, Elizabeth, New Jersey, Murphy and Dana, 1918*
10. *View of Archibald Bull Housing*

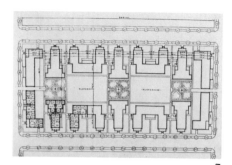

7

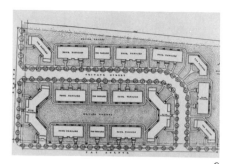

9

8

FAY AVENUE, TO HOUSING DEVELOPMENT AT ELIZABETH, N. J
Murphy & Dana, Architects.

10

The Sunnyside project, designed by Stein and Henry Wright in 1924, consists of several two- and four-story grouped houses aligned parallel to the street. Each home has a private front and rear entrance and a small private back yard which opens onto a common area at the center of the block. Sunnyside does not present a home-like image, however. The street facade is long, relentless and unfortunately institutional in its appearance. This can be partly attributed to the fact that Stein was limited to a two hundred foot deep New York block. But although Stein did not have the opportunity at Sunnyside to place his buildings with their long dimension perpendicular to the street, other semi-urban projects built under the same constraints did manage to convey an image of domesticity which is missing at Sunnyside. Murphy and Dana's Archibald Bull housing development in Elizabeth, New Jersey (1918) was a well-publicized example of this type.[13]

The real estate collapse of 1926 and the stock market failure of 1929 slowed the growth of America's suburbs even if they did not quell the ideal. "America's Little House," we should remember, was not built until 1934. But when, in the mid-1940's, the suburbanizing of America recommenced in earnest, economic and social conditions no longer favored the development of free-standing group housing of the type proposed by Jacobs and Stein during the early 1920's. The economic island which had existed between the tenement and the suburbs had been swallowed by the combined tides of government-funded urban housing and the rationalized, open-market production of the American single-family home.

[1]"The Second New York Own-Your-Home Exposition", Building Age, vol. 42, June 1920, p. 50.

[2]New York Times, May 18, 1919, p. 1, " 'Own Your Home' Show" see also "The Second New York Own-Your-Home Exposition", *Building Age,* vol. 42, June 1920, p. 50-52.

[3]Stein, C.S., Transcript of the Commission of Housing and Regional-Planning—Tax Exemption Hearings, 1924, p. 3.

[4]See Stein, C.S., *Toward New Towns for America,* MIT Press, Cambridge, 1956 also Mumford, Lewis, *Sketches from Life,* The Dial Press, New York, 1982, p. 336-346. For the Architects' Small House Service Bureau of the United States, see Architects' Small House Service Bureau of the United States Inc., *Small Homes of Architectural Distinction,* New York, 1929.

[5]Ford, James, *America's Little House,* Better Homes in America, Inc., New York, 1934, foreword.

[6]Bauer, Catherine and Jacob Crane, "What Every Family Should Have", *Survey Graphic,* vol. 29, no. 2, Feb. 1940, New York.

[7]Ford, James, *op. cit.*

[8]Stein, C.S., *Commission of Housing and Regional Planning—Tax Exemption Hearings,* unpublished minutes from the Henry Wright Library, Feb. 20, 1924.

[9]Testimony by Louis Gold, New York builder, and Harry R. Gilbert, advertising agent representing building operators of Queens, before Commission of Housing..., Stein, C.S., *op. cit.*

[10]"The Metropolitan Houses in Long Island City," Architecture and Building, vol. 56, May 1924, p. 42-44, plates, also "Metropolitan Life Ready to build $9-a-Room Apartments," Real Estate Record and Guide, June 24, 1922, p. 775.

[11]New York Times, May 14, 1919, p. 3.

[12]Stein proposed the housing of 92 families on a 3.2 acre site. Boyd, John Taylor, Jr., "Garden Apartments in Cities," *The Architectural Record,* vol. 48, n. 1, July 1920, p. 71.

[13]Fisher, Boyd, "Good Housing as a Reducer of Labor Turnover", National Housing Association Publications, New York, 1919. The Archibald Bull project houses 54 families on two and one fifth acres.

**Formalism Follows Functionalism:
Critical Attitudes Towards
Post-War American Architecture**
Sheryl L. Kolasinski

After World War II, the American architectural community was faced with a unique opportunity and responsibility. A generation of American architects had been educated by the immigrant modern masters and the unprecedented building boom following the Depression and war years gave them the chance to put their lessons into practice.

While the "building" of theories may inevitably stray from the rigor of the initial conceptions, the post-war American building experience took place in social, economic and cultural circumstances far removed from those in which the precepts of modern architecture grew. The fundamental notion of functionalism was transformed in America. As Sibyl Moholy-Nagy has observed,

> To the Bauhaus masters and to Le Corbusier, function was ideology, the visual prophecy of a better, purer social order...To the American builder, Functionalism was a formula guaranteeing the most advantageous ratio between investment and profit return...free of any sociological implications.[1]

Thus, if the formal principles and methods of the modern movement could be applied to architecture in the United States, the meaning of that architecture was changed by the nature of the circumstances of its production and ideology. This left to critics and historians the task of assessing the formalism of the American architectural contribution and the discovery of what was specifically American about that production.

In his review of the developments leading to the American architecture of the fifties, Vincent Scully suggests that up to 1949, American architectural theory was "non-existent" and that "architecture as a topic of gene-

ral urbanistic meaning almost ceased to exist".[2] In characteristically crisp and straightforward style, Scully states that a false opposition had been set up between International Style (Walter Gropius, Marcel Breuer) and Bay Region (Harwell Harris, William Wurster) suburban houses, between an organic, intuitive, native art and an inorganic, thoughtful, fine art. Dismissing these distinctions, Scully contends that the leading characteristic of early modern American architecture, as during the American Beaux-Arts period, is pictorialism.[3]

Pictorialism is not only an American characteristic to Scully, but one long associated with the International Style. Among the formal qualities embodied by pictorialism are

> subtle transparencies, the diminution of scale, the play of very thin planes—...flow, change and ambiguity...(not) monumentality.[4]

In discovering this pictorial quality, Scully's critical method mirrors his subject. He examines Breuer and Belluschi's American work (in comparison to Le Corbusier) as if they were isolated art objects, commenting on their "graphic sensibility"[5], their likeness to Paul Klee's and Laszlo Moholy-Nagy's works, their lack of empathy with the human figure.

Sibyl Moholy-Nagy is an observor and critic who retained a nostalgia for the heroic beginnings of the modern movement. Nonetheless, in several essays written between 1953 and 1970, she comes to some conclusions similar to Scully's. When discussing the work of Paul Rudolph, she identifies "the specifically American preference for visual rather than rational values".[6] Furthermore, "the appearance of technological building materials and mechanical equipment..in America..became imme-

diately ornamental".[7]

Moholy-Nagy, however, cannot be dismissed as a formalist critic. She applies the standards of the founding fathers of the Modern Movement to the works she examines and rails against "preciousness, academism, historical ignorance and lack of social consciousness".[8] With the clear criteria of modernism as her critical tools, she finds in 1950's American houses a uniquely American need, "the Architectural definition of a native environment".[9] Evidence for this is found in the early work of Paul Rudolph, whose Florida houses temper the rigorous forms of modernism with climatic considerations. Not a regional style in the sense of the vernacular, Rudolph's "regional adjustment is spatial and atmospheric".[10]

Rudolph's work becomes emblematic of the promise and problems of American modernism for other critics as well. Both William H. Jordy and Peter Collins, respectively, cite Rudolph among the architects striving for individualistic expression within the framework of the new classical formalism or within the stylistically eclectic (or ambiguous) designation "form-giver".

In "The Formal Image: U.S.A.", Jordy makes a case for why America had become the site of the most notable examples of the "drift" towards classicistic formalism.[11] First, technological innovations made the elegant Miesian vision of the machine a practical reality and a formal prototype. Then, a renewed interest in ornament contributed to the transformation of the Miesian aesthetic and helped to reconcile "individuality and correctness". Added to these are the "longing for historical association" (not the same as discovery or recovery of one's own history) and the dilution of "the sense of impersonality" that a "humanistic" neo-classic look provides.

Among the works Jordy employs to make his point are buildings by Rudolph, Philip Johnson, Edward Durell Stone, Gordon Bunshaft and Minoru Yamasaki. As a result of the collision of their formal concerns with functional requirements, Jordy finds elements of a "mannerist tension" in their works. The terms he uses to describe them are familiar both in the art historical sense of describing work of the sixteenth century and as the stock-in-trade of contemporary formalist critics: ambiguity, instability, layering, attenuation, exoticism.

Jordy clearly relishes the historian's task of delineating the new style, exposing its main features and putting it in an historical context. But as a critic, he spells out his reservations as well. If post-war American architecture had become influential "explicitly for the specific visual ideas (embodied)", it could also become so formally

> generalized and so suave that (it was) readily refined from the realm of experience to that of mere appropriateness.[12]

Jordy's implicit concern for the immediacy and genuineness of modern architecture as it expresses the American condition makes him wary of architecture which is "rationalized in terms of a nexus of function, novelty and tradition".[13]

These issues of novelty and relation to tradition concern Peter Collins as well. On the one hand, Collins criticizes Rudolph for designing "as if no architectural vocabulary existed"[14], and on the other, derides the historian's usual position that every work

forms a link in the chain of architectural development and... must therefore have some classifiable elements of novelty if the theory of evolution is to have any validity in the domain of art.[15]

Collins, like Jordy, is an historian, but with a different, polemical position. His critique of post-war American architecture is not only a critique of formalism, but also of the way in which that architecture is studied and classified. To him, architecture should be understood (as the nineteenth century did) as

> quite different from painting and sculpture in that the evolution of its forms, being based on technology and planning requirements, is best studied in terms of structural systems and building types.[16]

Collins' concern for the tectonic and typological aspects of architecture makes him impatient with the "Madison Avenue euphemism", form-giver. The emphasis on personality and novelty that this term implies does nothing to mitigate "the most pressing architectural problem facing North America today...chaotic individualism".[17]

Writing at the beginning of the 1960's, Collins begins to voice a number of that decade's critical concerns. His essays are among the least descriptive and most prescriptive of those surveyed here. Collin's criticism is the least impressionistic, the least reflective of the pictorialism and formalism he studies.

All of the essayists reviewed implicitly understand that once functionalism as an ideology has been subsumed beneath efficient-looking and technologically advanced building as a product, the formal innovations of the Modern Movement were

what remained. The works of contemporary architects are, therefore, judged by the formal criteria of the Modern Movement, and little reference to previously developed American traditions, or to America's tradition of the new, is made. The separation of methodology and ideology is apparent in both the architecture and criticism of post-war, post-functionalist America; it is where they converge that concern for the merely formal is transcended.

[1] Sibyl Moholy-Nagy, *The Architecture of Paul Rudolph,* New York, 1960, p. 7.

[2] Vincent Scully, "Doldrums in the Suburbs", *Journal of the Society of Architectural Historians,* March 1965, p. 36.

[3] *Ibid.,* p. 38.

[4] *Ibid.,* p. 39.

[5] *Ibid.,* p. 40.

[6] Sibyl Moholy-Nagy, "The Future of the Past", *Perspecta* 7, 1961, p. 73.

[7] *Ibid.,* p. 72.

[8] Sibyl Moholy-Nagy, "Victories and Defeats of Modern Architecture", *Progressive Architecture,* April 1953, p. 20.

[9] Moholy-Nagy, "Future of the Past", p. 73.

[10] Moholy-Nagy, *Rudolph,* p. 10.

[11] William H. Jordy, "The Formal Image: U.S.A.", *Architectural Review,* March 1960, p. 159.

[12] *Ibid.,* p. 160—162.

[13] *Ibid.*

[14] Peter Collins, "Whither Paul Rudolph?", *Progressive Architecture,* August 1961, p. 130.

[15] Peter Collins, "Historicism", *Architectural Review,* April 1960, p. 101.

[16] Peter Collins, "The Form-Givers", *Perspecta 7,* 1961, p. 91.

[17] Collins, "Rudolph", p. 133.

Teaching: A Critique of the Gropius Method
Klaus Herdeg

This material appears courtesy of the MIT Press. It is excerpted from The Decorated Diagram: Harvard Architecture and the Failure of the Bauhaus Legacy *by Klaus Herdeg to be published by the MIT Press later this year.*

My principle argument is that architectural training at Harvard under Gropius and Breuer strongly promoted—unconsciously, perhaps—the kinds of design decisions that shaped the buildings [of Harvard graduates]. Aside from actual student work produced in Gropius's and Breuer's studios, which would require patient historical research to find and catalog (for another kind of study), the best evidence to substantiate my thesis is curriculum objectives, as conveyed explicity and implicity, intentionally and unintentionally, in the catalog descriptions of courses and in the formulations of studio problems.

A closer examination of one of these, a sketch problem given to the master's class in 1950 by Gropius (assisted by Benjamin Thompson) and again, in slightly altered form, in 1951 (assisted by William Lyman), reveals an underlying design attitude that informed both school problems and commissioned buildings. The 1951 version, ''Site Development for Family Residences'' includes the following instructions:

The student is asked to select a 3-bedroom house of his liking, one he has designed or a plan by another, and on the site chosen explore the possibilities of achieving *visual variety* [italics mine] by such means as the following:
a. Use alternately the plan as well as its mirror.
b. Place the house at different angles to the sun.
c. Alternate the materials, their textures and colors, and alternate the bright and dark effect.
d. Confine the adjacent outdoor living space around the house by varying combinations of pergolas, trellis [sic], screens, hedges, fences, shrubs, and groups of trees.
e. Place the garage or car port at different angles to the house.
f. Add a screen porch to the house at different positions and angles.
To a large degree this means thinking creatively more about the spaces outside the house than those inside. The blunt extreme, where seemingly the former are never thought about, is the average speculative development which in growing numbers obliterates the American landscape.[1]

Presumably, the exercise is meant to stimulate the formulation of an answer to the deplored ''average speculative development''. It contains an invitation to think creatively about surrounding spaces, to be sure, but on what level, using what means? By considering the exterior spaces as potential extensions of interior spaces? By considering the spaces defined between two or more houses? No! The clue given the student is a list of pattern and texture elements pertaining to a *single* house in which house, garage, porch, trellises, hedges, and surface materials all assume equal importance. A preoccupation with pattern and texture seems to govern all scales from the site plan to the wood grain of a trellis. The very lack of hierachy among the items on the list confirms that preoccupation.

In point *d* the student is asked to confine outdoor areas. But instead of directing him to principles by which this might be done, such as degrees and methods of spatial enclosure, the exercise gives him a shopping list of predetermined objects and surface treatments. There is no reason for the student, following these instructions, to go beyond achieving a nice arrangement of objects and surfaces elements in the service of ''visual variety'', for he is asked to provide optical stimulation almost as an end in itself. The presentation requirement of ''perspective sketches showing the variety of appearances in spite of using the same house type''[2] reinforces that attitude. Thus, what was meant as an exercise in ''reconciling the economic advantages of mass production of standardized building parts with man's desire for individuality''[3]—a rather good objective, then and now—turned out to be a prescription for almost meaningless production of visual variety. The disturbing conclusion one must draw from this example is that the student was required to do no more than a visually appealing alternative to the speculator's development, the antithesis of the stated objective of the problem, while he was led to believe that he was bringing the world—or at least the American suburbs—one step closer to Bauhaus perfection. The reputation of his professor alone would have had him believe that.

The apparent contradiction between intentional and unintentional objectives has even larger implications. It is in a student problem like this one that we can perceive the seeds of formalism, in the pejorative sense as the term is commonly being used, that is, connoting the employment of forms for purely literal and superficial reasons such as visual variety. Formalism in this sense implies a total nonrecognition of the multiplicity of meanings a form may have: intrinsically, as part of a structure or system of forms or a fragment of imagined or real whole; iconographically, as a cultural symbol; and empirically, as a functional clue. One could, of course, make a case *for* formalism as connoting the deliberate employment of forms in the service of a larger conception of architecture which permits forms to function as repositories and generators of all levels of meaning—as agents of formal structure. Such an inversion would imply a recognition of certain immutable formal characteristics which are inherent in any form, solid or void, and its capacity, by means of formal analogies, to sponsor human activity, physical structure and construction techniques rather than be their by-product. Jefferson's University of Virginia is a vivid example of this kind of positive formalism, as are Colquhoun and Miller's school in London, Schinkel's Altes Museum in Berlin, Aalto's Villa Mairea in Finland, and Le Corbusier's Errazuris House in Chile, as well as his Villa in Vaucresson. Main Street is also a good example.

Expanding our search for clues to possible curriculum intentions (both explicit and implicit) beyond the examination of one representative master's class problem, we can indentify three characteristics which permeate the curriculum as it is represented in the official course descriptions and in a random selection of master's class problems. The first is an explicit *commitment to architecture in the service of democratic ideals;* the second is an implicit *preference for suburbia* over the city as the proper locale for human habitation; and the third is a *bias in favor of pragmatism.* These form an underlying value structure, a philosophical and aesthetic attitude toward architectural design with a concomitant distrust of history and theory. (All three characteristics are evident, in varying degrees of intensity and mixture, in the work of the Harvard graduates.) Anyone familiar with Gropius's writings, as collected in *Scope of Total Architecture,* will understand these attitudes as a further expression of beliefs which he never tired of asserting all through his Bauhaus and Harvard years. There is, of course, some irony in finding such a sharply delineated attitude permeating a curriculum which was meant to foster open-mindedness among its students. As Walter Gropius said when he took over the chairmanship at Harvard:

> It is not so much a ready-made dogma that I want to teach, but an attitude towards the problems of our generation which is unbiased, original and elastic.[4]

Perhaps the very loftiness of such ideals increases the distance between intention and solution by loading from the start heavy burdens of conscience and social responsibilities on every design decision. All the more so since generalized, abstract goals do not by definition lend themselves to interpretation and transformation in designing buildings. On the other hand, models, be they buildings, trees or poems, equipped with their formal structures, permit the invention of analogous formal structures suited to the task at hand. It was Gropius's wish, it seems, to eliminate the notion of the model altogether. Yet the human proclivity to perceive and think in object (model) terms made his directives vague and the field for design action foggy. Models or model types, at least architectural ones, are unlikely to be suggested in a studio problem conceived of in an anti-historical attitude, for the very concept of modeling relies on precedent, if not on history in an academic sense. Memory as much as aspiration is touched by models, making a structured yet individualized design process possible. Yet, despite the history-free appearance of the design directives given to Harvard students, which implied the possibility, if not the certainty, of entirely original solutions, two types— ''good'' modern movement buildings and ''bad'' academic buildings—could still insinuate themselves into the problem formulation, thereby undercutting the intended aim.

[1]''Site Development for Family Residences,'' Master's Class Problem, 1951.
[2]*Ibid.*
[3]*Ibid.*
[4]Leonardo Benevolo, *History of Modern Architecture,* Cambridge, Mass., 1971, pp. 652-653.

The Progressive Uses of Tradition
Jon Michael Schwarting

This article is in part excerpted from Rome: A Study of Urban Formation and Transformation *by Michael Schwarting, Rizzoli International, to be published later this year.*

1. Comparison of Villa Foscari and Villa Stein
2. Aerial view of the Louvre

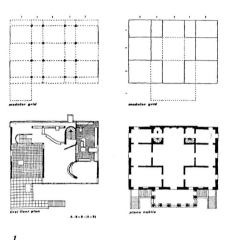

1

2

The association of conservative values with the notion of tradition is so commonplace as to be generally taken for granted. A progressive use of tradition appears as an untenable contradiction if one accepts this association. The concept of stasis is embodied in the idea of tradition just as the concept of change is essential to that of progress. In a dialectical discourse, it is possible to suggest that progress or change is dependent on its antithesis, tradition or stasis. Stasis is that by which one measures and that which stimulates change. Given the dialectical relationshiop between stasis and change, tradition and progress, it is viable to pursue this notion specifically in terms of the form and content of architecture.

One definition of formalism in architecture, or formal analysis of architectural proposals (as this is probably the only realm where pure formalism can exist), is the preoccupation with the classifying of forms and their relations with regard to their physical, perceptual and psychological effects. It is a search for eternally valid generalizations which exist outside history. Attempts to classify forms into types of forms have, however, generally proceeded with an analysis of their historical application. An ability to construct new forms or a new formal language, to paraphrase Alan Colquhoun, "would have to presuppose the language itself".[1]

Without analyzing the history of the actual application of forms, we are left with such meager findings as Rudolph Arnheim's analysis of the psycho-physical characteristics of a square, circle, balance, equilibrium, etc. Arnheim himself illustrates these concepts with historical examples to confirm them. Unless we can postulate an extremely complex "scientific" extention of Arnheim's classifications to encompass all forms that can be analyzed from history, we must base our selection of forms on a knowledge of the history of their use and the needs they were used to answer. We will transform them to resolve present problems if we are progressive; we will retreat into a reconstitution of tradition if we are conservative. We remain in a state described by Julian Guadet in his *Elements et Theories de l'Architecture* of 1909: that of envisaging all centuries and countries as a reservoir of possible motifs of composition; [the architect] is able to deduce certain broad conclusions, to rediscover in all periods the presence of a common denominator which is conceived as transcending style.[2] (*1*)

Working with preexisting formal and compositional modes in and of itself cannot be proclaimed to be either conservative or progressive. It is the interface between the selection of forms and the problems which they are intended to address, what Paul Frankl termed "purposeful intention", that relates formal composition to conservative or progressive tendencies. This does not mean that forms are inconsequential to meaning, but rather that they are either conservative or progressive only in terms of their relationship to technological, production, economic and social issues.

Architecture works not only with abstract form, with a formal typology from which forms are selected for specific ends, but also with a social typology. This typology consists in both social and architectural history of socio-cultural institutions such as libraries, schools, jails, and single family homes. These institutions are created by society to reinforce its ideology, their traditions of established custom, practice and ways of thinking. Through these institutions, tradition attains the status of unwritten law, or reality itself.

Since the program is essentially provided by society in these institutions, the architect is not given the material and mandate to explore progressive change unless there is a demand for the reevaluation of existing institutions or the invention of new

3. *Perspective view of the Famili-stere, Guise, France*
4. *"Redent" apartment blocks by Le Corbusier*

ones. With little control over the program, the architect, as any individual, has the option to accept or reject given institutions and their ideological meaning. Without a consensus on this issue in society, the architect must either work with statements and proposals or must create work with a double reading. The architect is in jeopardy of, on the one hand, losing the work by not being properly accomodating or, on the other, being too subtle and not achieving the hidden agenda of communicating the second reading.

Any attempt to make an existing ideology transparent, to expose, interpret or possibly alter it, requires references to the existing traditional mode in order to argue the point. Furthermore, through an analysis of history, it is possible not only to understand how a social system has operated and realized itself, but also to determine how to transform its expressions to new ends. The very fact of a form's connection and acceptance within a normative traditional meaning could be a critical source of its power, impact and acceptance as a proposal for change.

For example, Louis XIV achieved a certain autocratic power through the development of the capitalist class system and produced Versailles and the Louvre as demonstrations of that power. As such, the forms and images of these buildings should not be decried and expunged from progressive consciousness. (*2*) The accrued meaning and impact of these building images could be transferred to a new cause. That the Familistere by Godin at Guise, France, a Fourierian Phalanstery, has a configuration like that of the Louvre is part of its intended power to attract. (*3*)

3

Fourier outlined the physical attributes of his communal settlement; it was modelled on the layout of Versailles, its central wing being given over to public functions (dining hall, library, wintergarden, etc.) while its side wings were devoted to the workshops and the 'caravansary' ... He saw it as a structure whose grandeur, if generally adopted, would replace the petit-bourgeoise squalor of the small, individual free-standing houses that were, by then, already filling the outer interstices of towns.[3]

Le Corbusier's housing proposal of the 1920's not only made sense as a minimum dwelling, with real amenities for the mass population, but also derived its force as well as its connection to traditional culture through its formal relationship to the Louvre. Its form assisted the potential acceptance of the *Une Maison-Une Palais* socio-political concept. (*4*) Le Corbusier argued for certain honorific elements such as terraces in the sky, double height volumes and free plan as well as an image for the dwelling of the under class of industrial society which

4

could metaphorically replace that of the upper class palace. Through its relationship to tradition, as a transformation of an image, this was a very different approach to housing than the lowest common denominator minimum dwelling. As such, it has sustained meaning today.

It would seem that we ought to try to establish a value system which takes account of the forms and solutions of the past if we are to gain control over concepts which will obtrude themselves into the creative process, whether we like it or not... My purpose is not to advocate a reversion to an architecture which accepts tradition unthinkingly. This would imply that there was fixed and immutable relation between forms and meaning. The characteristic of our age is change, and it is precisely because this is so that it is necessary to investigate the part which modifications of type-solutions play in relation to problems and solutions which are without precedent in any received tradition.[4]

5. *House by Richard Norman Shaw*
6. *Watts-Sherman House. Site plan*
7. *Watts-Sherman House. West elevation*
8. *Watts-Sherman House. First floor plan and axonometric*

(Drawings by J. Bartelstone, B. Holden, and D. Rotholz)

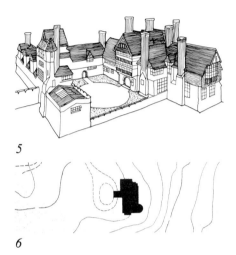

5

6

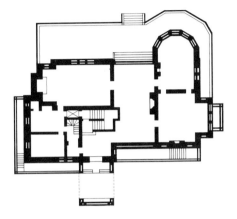

7

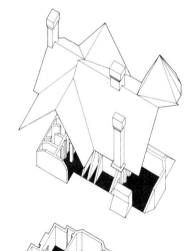

8

Many examples of this dialectical concept of the progressive uses of tradition could be discussed. Aspects of this discussion were carried out in the first year Principles of Architecture course (fall 1982) at a presentation of two student analysis projects.

H.H. Richardson's Watts-Sherman house in Newport, Rhode Island (*5, 6, 7 and 8*) was build in 1874-5 for an upper class doctor. Stanford White worked on the project in Richardson's office and later made additions to it himself. It is a house with twelve bedrooms, seven of which are for servants who work in the basement and live in the attic. Twenty-five years later, in 1900, Frank Lloyd Wright designed a "Home in a Prairie Town" for the Ladies Home Journal. (*9, 10 and 11*) It was to be sold for $7,000. This house has four to six bedrooms, one or two possibly for servants.

Both houses have essentially pinwheel plan organizations. The Richardson house has an "L" shaped center hall containing a vestibule, stair and large fireplace. This forms a central pivoting piece. To this are ap-pended the living room, dining room and library as well as the port-cochere, entry and back terrace. These rooms are stately, closed, axial and symmetrical in organization and mimic, although in a smaller form, typical upper class European fifteenth to nineteenth century residences.

Wright's house also has a pinwheel organization. Rather than closed rooms, Wright's rooms, which are smaller than Richardson's, are more open and read as a single articulated volume as much as individual entities. These public rooms borrow from each other to achieve grandeur.

Richardson masks his house with an image of Richard Norman Shaw's nineteenth century Queen Anne style of upper class England. The Medieval "Hall", with a large scale fireplace and richly decorated rooms, work with the external volumetrics to convey the elegance of the life of the privileged class. Richardson and White devoted their careers to the maintenance and stabilization of this way of life.

On the other hand, Wright was very interested in the growth and stabilization of the middle class, the

9. *Home in a Prairie Town. First floor plan, Second floor plan and perspective*
10. *Home in a Prairie Town. Section and front elevation*
11. *Home in a Prairie Town. Site plan*

(Drawings by S. Greenwald, J. Mejias, and W. Shugart)

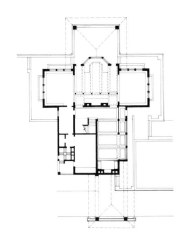

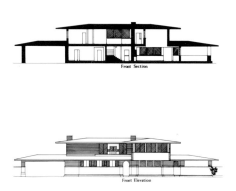

10

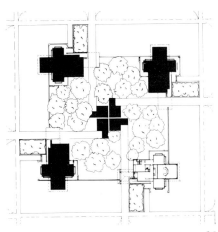

11

9

managerial backbone of the American capitalist system. His houses celebrate the suburb, the semi-autonomy of private property and the automobile. Instead of servants, the wife is placed in the back of the house in the kitchen. Wright's interest in working for the middle class had its effect on his formal and spatial invention. The spatial flow and efficiency of his plans, derived from the "destruction of the box", is brought about, to some degree, by the fact that he was designing under economic constraints which dictated smaller spaces and simpler construction techniques than those Richardson used.

The pinwheel itself has limited meaning. Each of these houses opposed classicism from separate viewpoints. One refers to a medieval tradition of articulation of pieces or functions, organized by aspects of the French classical tradition of local symmetries. Wright's attitude comes from a nineteenth century romantic metaphor of the "seed", "germ" or growth with its nascent existential sensibility. By making a plan that pinwheels around the large central fireplace, Wright denies the Renaissance

salon as metaphor of cortile or center and man must now occupy the periphery eccentric to the whole.

Richardson's manipulation of tradition in terms of form and image is inventive but is socially conservative. His rooms repeat a tradition. Wright goes further beyond tradition, combining the informal pinwheel with a formal rigor of local symmetry in such a way that the commensurate invention of spatial division has a new social meaning. It is, as Richardson transformed the image of Shaw's England to a more pragmatic American object, a transformation of a tradition which implanted a new tradition.

[1] Colquhoun, Alan, "Typology and the Design Method", *Essays in Architectural Criticism: Modern Architecture and Historical Change,* Cambridge, Mass., 1982, p. 49.
[2] Rowe, Colin, "The Mathematics of the Ideal Villa", *Architectural Review,* March 1947, p. 102.
[3] Frampton, Kenneth, *Modern Architecture: A Critical History,* New York 1980, p. 22.
[4] Colquhoun, p. 49.

First Year Studio
Master of Architecture
Spring 1982
Urban Community Center
Wiebke Noack
Critic: Alex Kouzmanoff
First year, spring 1982

1. Plan
2. Axonometric

At least four different ethnic groups live here on the Lower East Side of Manhattan. Their community represents an American ideal, a place where an individual will find acceptance and liberty. In reality, an urban place can separate people by ethnicity and age. The Community Center should be a place that transcends urban isolation and motivates a heightened sense of neighborhood.

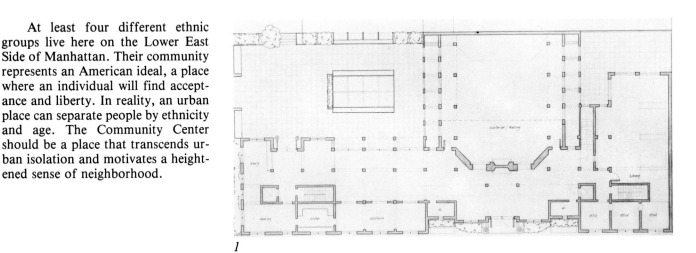

1

2

1. *First floor plan*
2. *Third floor plan*
3. *Axonometric*

Urban Community Center
Jay Vigoreaux
Critic: Barbara Littenberg
First year, spring 1982

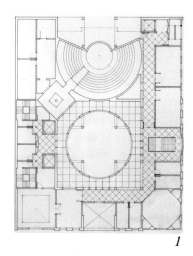

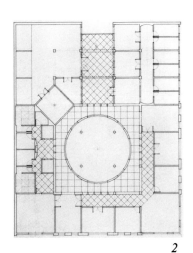

In this scheme, compatible programmatic elements are organized horizontally around a circular courtyard in the form of a traditional rotunda. This is the focus of the composition—a public, covered plaza that functions both as a forum for the community it serves and as a referential space to which users can relate at any floor level. The rotunda form as part of the facade expresses the building's public character and may become a symbol of the adjacent community.

1

2

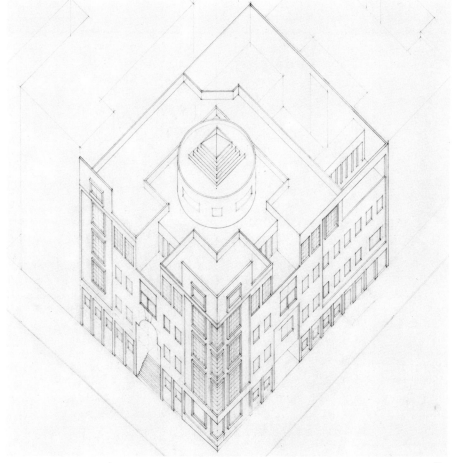

3

Urban Community Center
Daniel Monk
Critic: Dimitri Balamotis
First year, spring 1982

1. East Broadway elevation
2. First floor plan
3. Longitudinal section

The design of the center was based on a consideration of the morphological context and the location of institutions providing similar services within a five-block radius of the site.

The crucial corner of the street wall facing Seward Park was reconstituted. Here, a monumental stair leading to a public room, or community forum, was placed. In response to client preference for privacy, entrances to specific functions (center for the aged, health services and gymnasium) run along the periphery of the site. Storefronts along East Broadway are connected to job-training workshops below.

The conscious decentralization is resolved at the semi-public garden at the center of the site, the swimming pool, directly below the garden, is also conceived of as a primary space. The pool is a ''draw'', an attraction for this center which is complementary to the theater complex and gym provided by the two other social service agencies in the area.

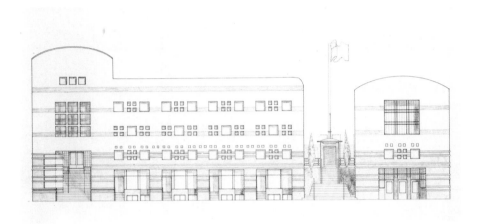

1

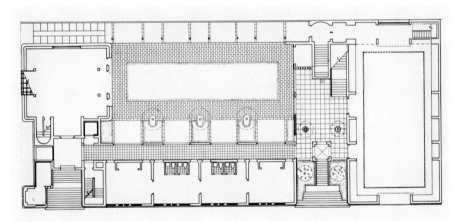

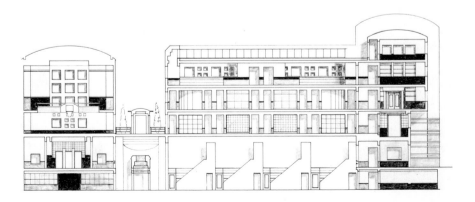

2

3

1. *Wong: Elevation*
2. *Wong: Interior perspective*
3. *Chia: Axonometric*

Urban Community Center
Jarvis Wong
Critic: John James
Chia Yin Hsu
Critic: Dimitri Balamotis
First year, spring 1982

1

2

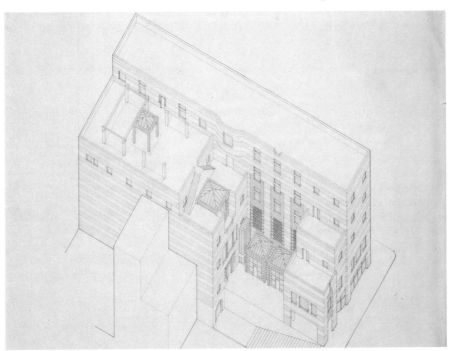

3

Wong: This Community Center, located at Broadway and 115th Street in Manhattan, has a monumental facade in response to its immediate surroundings. This monumental aspect is repeated in the double height, skylit lobby. The lobby, in turn, gives onto the main public forum/exhibition space.

Chia: the edge conditions of the courtyard organize this scheme: one side is insulated from the street by the spine of the building, another filters out to the street through a gateway, another opens completely to the adjacent amphitheater. Alternating bands of color on the facades reinforce the sense of continuity from one volume of the sculptural whole to another.

Hostel in the Southern Berkshires
Peter Pennoyer
Critic: John James
First year, spring 1982

1. Site plan
2. North and south elevations
3. Upper and lower plans

1

The site for this fifty-guest hostel encompasses a roadside pasture and wooded hill in the Berkshire mountains of southwestern Massachusetts. The buildings are situated in a clearing at the top of the site, visible from the road without disturbing the pasture below. The hostel's siting takes advantage of both the local river and the broad views over the valley beyond.

The main building—a great shingled lodge—recalls the character of the local farm buildings, but conveys a more formal attitude. The lodge's shape and its relationship to the administrator's residence create three orientations: the main portion of the hostel faces the terraced gaming lawns; the vaulted living room faces the river; the house has views of its own gardens. On the upper floor, each guest room has a southern exposure and projecting bays at the kitchen and entry hall create lighted seating areas on the ground floor.

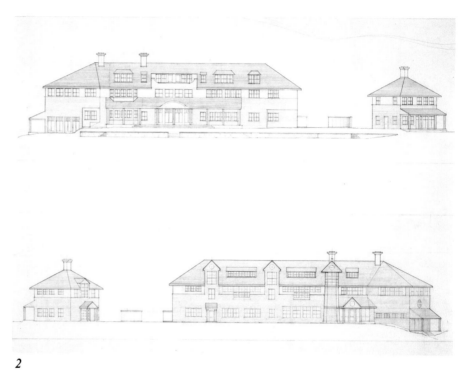

2

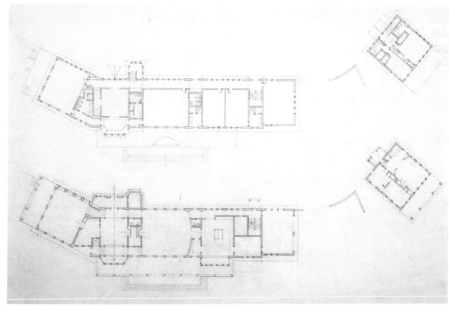

3

1. *Lower plan and elevation*
2. *Site plan*

Hostel in the Southern Berkshires
Ted Krueger
Critic: Michael Schwarting
First year, spring 1982

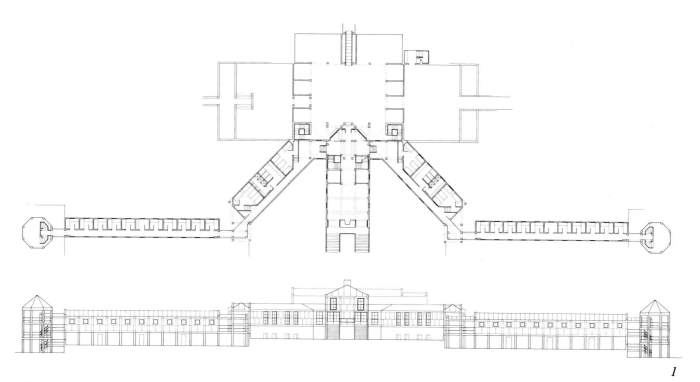

1

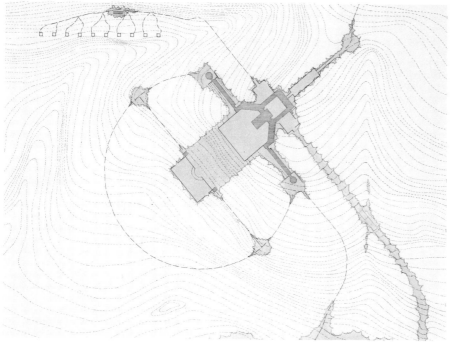

2

The aggregation of painted white wooden buildings in the landscape is characteristic of New England farm complexes. A classical formal intention is evident in much of the vernacular architecture of the area. In the relationship between objects and landscape neither dominates, but a gentle opposition serves to reinforce and define each.

The same relationship is sought by the interventions proposed here, but is obtained by different means. The plan of the complex is reminiscent of a royal compound and the principal facade is symmetrical and hierarchical. However, the scale and the materials, plywood on foundations of local stone, are modest. The proportions, disposition of masses and relationship of wall to opening, rather than details, are derived from the classical language.

Hostel in the Southern Berkshires
Charles Anderson
Critic: Michael Schwarting
First year, spring 1982

1. *Axonometric*
2. *Lower plan*
3. *Upper plan*

Walls, stairways and terraces are carved out of the hillside to define a procession through the site. A central hearth establishes a core; to either side, communal living and dining spaces project onto large grass terraces. Each of two sleeping quarters borders a terrace and therefore is linked to the projected communal spaces. A pinwheel deck floats above the carved landscape, intersecting each of the buildings differently to create sleeping porches, meeting rooms and a central outdoor cooking area. Interior and exterior open spaces overlap through use of sliding wall panels of wood and glass. The central hearth interlocks solid earth and floating structure.

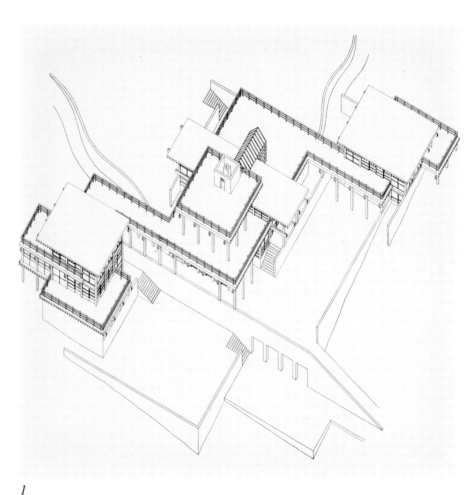

1

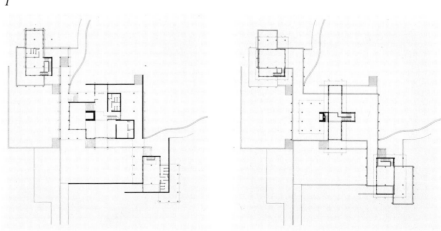

2   3

1. *Goldblum: Axonometric*
2. *Heim: Axonometric*

Hostel in the Southern Berkshires
Michael Goldblum
Critic: Dimitri Balamotis
Laura Heim
Critic: Ghislaine Hermanuz
First year, spring 1982

1

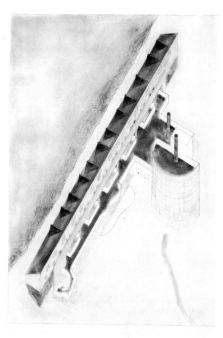

2

Goldblum: My intention was to create a lost city, a village to be discovered, tripped upon by the traveling camper. In trying to understand the elements which identify and characterize the American village (around here, at least), I looked not only to colonial towns and their constituent parts, but also to our early college campuses, which were at once physical reductions and conceptual idealizations of this country's cities. By referring to and fragmenting these precedents, I would hope first, to recommend to the hostellers that spirit of community and pioneering which empowered those designs, and second, to suggest that their method of creation is still viable, potentially expressive of new ideas while remaining rich in associations and meaning for our society.

Heim: This project seeks to define the edge between a mountainous forest of dense, vertical elements and an open, horizontal valley. The lower, linear organization of individual rooms, partially concealed from the road by a screen, lies under the canopy of trees. The screen acts as a backdrop for the collective spaces which are bold objects in the open field. The built forms act as a counterpoint to the characteristics of the landscape, while acknowledging the nature of the activities within them. Bridges link the two sides, forming a place from which to recognize the two realms.

Urban Housing for the Eighties:
The High Rise Block with
Common Services
Michael Mostoller

1. Boarding house room

A severe struggle for control of the urban territory is now taking place in New York City. It is a struggle between rich and poor, families and single people, mannered society and outcasts. And it is focused on the single-room occupancy hotel (SRO), the residence of poor, single men and women, and the commercial loft building, the home of many small manufacturing concerns. Both building types are ideal for conversion to luxury housing.

Housing reform, since New York's tenement house law of 1867, has been directed toward the family dwelling. First efforts concentrated on eliminating health and safety hazards: bad water, poor sanitary conditions, overcrowding and fires. During the next fifty years, "new law" tenements replaced "old law" tenements, which replaced unregulated "tenant houses." By the 1930's, housing reformers had expanded their efforts to include the neighborhood and worked to eliminate the slum and develop new housing types. The focus of reform, however, always remained the family dwelling. And in a certain sense, this 100-year improvement process has been a success. For the majority of families, fair, decent and reasonably commodious housing is now available.

Yet while this chapter in housing reform may be closing, even a cursory inspection of our cities today lays bare a housing crisis of unforeseen dimensions, that of dwindling accommodations for the single adult, particularly the low-income adult. If the first strike against an individual in our society is low income, then within the ranks of the low-income single person vulnerability after vulnerability is found: old age, widowhood, physical handicaps, chronic histories

1. Boarding house room

1

of institutionalization and unemployment, and, indeed, homelessness itself. In New York City in 1983, an estimated 36,000 to 50,000 men and women live on the streets, about 200,000 women over 65 live alone, and over half of all households consists of one person (compared to 25% in 1970). In the dense urban core single person households are the rule, not the exception. In the entire country, urban and rural, approximately one quarter of the population now lives alone.

While the dimensions of the new chapter of the housing problem are seen in increasingly shocking proportions, we find that hidden within the "tenement" and "slum" problems is the lodger problem: the single person in search of housing. Indeed, New York City housing legislation began with lodging house regulations as early as 1676. Subsequent laws for lodging houses, enacted in 1799, 1804, 1848 and 1849, came before the tenement reform movement began.

Today, an interesting circle is drawn: the first recognition of housing problems began with the lodging house for single individuals. Three hundred years later, we return to the

same issue. In the intervening period, the lodger problem, though occasionally recognized as valid, was generally either considered evil in itself or degenerate in relation to family life or ignored while the tenement and slum problems were attacked.

The nineteenth century truly could be called the century of the boarding house. Its roots go back to the beginnings of American cities; for example, Thomas Jefferson is said to have stayed in his Washington boarding house on the day of his inauguration and took his customary meal there as well. During the nineteenth century the number of boarding houses greatly expanded to fulfill the vast new requirements born of rapid industrialization and subsequent urbanization. With its meal service and parlor, the boarding house allowed a single individual to live "privately, decently and economically".[1] The boarding house was an important part of urban life: in 1856, Walt Whitman estimated that three quarters of middle class New York either was boarding or took in boarders.[2]

Nevertheless, it was the tenement, not the boarding house, that benefited from nineteenth century

2. Mills Hotel, Ernest Flagg,
*   architect*
3. Typical floor, Mills Hotel

2

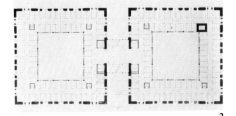

3

housed about 7000 men a night. The Municipal Lodging House on East 25th Street contained dormitories for 912 men, along with shower, fumigation, dining, laundry and health care facilities. In 1935, a Women's Building was provided on West 14th Street.

The most famous philanthropic endeavor of the era was the Mills Hotel, located on Bleeker Street between Sullivan and Thompson Streets. It opened in 1897 and housed 1000 men at ten cents a night each. The hotel was designed as a double series of rooms surrounding two great nine-story glazed courtyards, recalling the Familistere, the nineteenth century utopian scheme at Guise, France. Two other Mills hotels opened in subsequent years. Symptomatic of our contemporary "utopia," the first hotel was recently converted into luxury condomimiums and is called "The Atrium", that ubiquitous sign of modernity. The others are not operating or have been destroyed.

Institutional variations on this type, including YWCA's, YMCA's and the Salvation Army, have been developed all over the world. In addition, many private societies and institutions have provided homes for single men and women.

In the 20's and 30's, the rooming house replaced the boarding house. Generally without common services, it was an extremely degraded form of boarding house. With continued urbanization, an increased standard of living and the greatly increased density of the city, single person accommodations began to be constructed as a variation on the apartment and the hotel. Essentially, this meant a smaller apartment. The separate dining room was eliminated, the separate sleeping room was diminished or removed, and the kitchen greatly re-

duced. Like a hotel, a wide variety of communal services was offered at street level. This fusion of hotel service with permanent, minimal, often furnished rooms became known as the "apartment hotel." The New York City Building Code in 1924 defined an apartment hotel as any building in which the rooms were laid out in suites or apartments and the meals served from a main kitchen.

The American apartment hotel emerged as a type necessary for the modern metropolis. The on-going breakup of the family, which had been disguised in the growth of lodging and boarding houses, was finally acknowledged in the development of this new dwelling type. This truly 20th century form, the highrise apartment hotel, was a response to the increased status, wealth and independence of the single person.

A large number of low-income workers came into the city in search of jobs during World War II. This so strained the rooming house stock that another new building type emerged: the Single Room Occupancy Hotel, or SRO. It was a fusion of the two existing single-person housing strains, the lodging-boarding-rooming house and the hotel-apartment house.

While the rooming house of the 30's and 40's was most often occupied by poor, transient workers, low-income accommodations during the 50's began to house the unemployed, long-term resident.

By the middle fifties, an unplanned and unwilling interdependence between the Department of Welfare and the more marginal SRO's emerged. Both families and single people were referred to SRO's by welfare centers for temporary housing which tended to become permanent.[3]

housing reforms which were concerned with developing healthier environments and relieving overcrowding. These reforms included the expulsion of the lodger from the tenement, regardless of the fact that the lodger system was common and necessary in this housing economy. These housing reforms actually meant less housing for single people.

At the end of the century, local governments and philanthropic institutions began to build municipal lodging houses for poorer single men and women. By 1909, New York City

4. *Parkview Hotel*
5. *Mrs. H.'s room*
6. *Plan, Mrs. H.'s room*

4

5

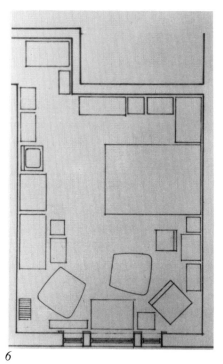

6

Other, more seriously disadvantaged individuals, "former prisoners, mental hospital dischargees and homeless convalescents from other hospitals"[4], were also referred to SRO's. Families were soon forbidden by council law in these buildings.

Alongside the formation of the SRO came the disappearance of large numbers of rooming houses. While the exact reasons for this can only be arrived at through further study, two possible contributing factors are:

1) the change of tenants from low-income white workers to an unemployed black/Hispanic urban "underclass" may have discouraged the small landlord from renting out the brownstone type;

2) more clearly, the urban renewal projects of the 1950's and 1960's simply destroyed the vast majority of them. Those buildings not razed were often converted back to upper-class family or studio apartments in the gentrification that followed urban renewal. The eradication of the housing stock for the low-income individual has continued throughout the 70's and 80's with the conversion of the SRO's to luxury accommodations. Within a very short

time, this forty-year old process of eliminating low-income, single adult housing may be complete.

There is another aspect of the problem that already has become tragic in scope. While the range of single housing types were being destroyed one by one, leaving virtually only the SRO and a totally inadequate emergency shelter system, another invisible housing type was being abandoned. This type, even more disguised than lodging in our customary view of housing, was revealed when 50,000 patients of the New York State mental health system were released. The asylum, of course, must be considered a housing type as well as an institution. Where they no longer function, a very difficult and volatile housing problem emerges. The "de-institutionalized" individual today may live in an SRO, the streets, or nowhere.

Housing for the single adult in our cities is further complicated by two other factors. The first, critical to the housing problem, is simple: our society is aging. The impact of this problem on housing can be seen in the proliferation of housing types for the elderly and the greater percentage of

our housing stock devoted to the elderly. Elderly housing, nursing homes, hospitals, "Independent Group Residences" and "Enriched Housing" for the frail elderly all testify to the new demands being made on our residential stock by the increase in the number of older people. And because, contrary to the myth of the married pair, older people most often live alone, the SRO is the last refuge of many elderly poor.

The other factor that further complicates the urban housing picture is an inflationary and high-interest-rate economy. The resulting pressure on housing prices is so acute that the small apartment is seen by developers as the wave of the future. Such real estate slogans as "The 300 sq. ft. home and other ideas for the eighties," "Small will be Smart" and "The boardinghouse will be back", suggest that the lodging or SRO type

7. *Proposed plan, Vera Institute*
   for Justice Apartment Hotel
8. *Sleeping rough*

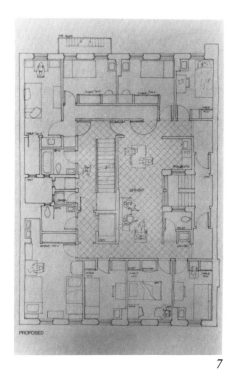

7

8

is being pre-empted by professionals and the upper-middle class. In New York this is currently reflected in the J-51 conversions that have cut the SRO stock from 50,000 to 19,000 units in five years.

We face a set of serious conditions. Lodging and rooming houses have vanished in all but one or two limited areas of New York City. The residential hotels for women are almost gone. Cheap hotels vanish at an increasing rate. The SRO is an "endangered species". The city shelters housed twice as many homeless men seventy years ago as they do now. This debilitated housing stock has had to absorb the individuals "of the asylum". The economic crunch is forcing middle and upper income renters into the lodger-SRO market. An enlarged need for single units for the elderly has developed.

History has indeed come full circle; the housing issue of the 1980's is the same as that of the 1780's. The "lodger problem" is still with us.

At Columbia University, we have attempted to address this problem in several ways. First, the Graduate School of Architecture and Planning joined an interdisciplinary curriculum development and services training project with the Schools of Social Work, Law, Medicine, Nursing and Dentistry. Within this program architecture students Bob Lane, Ray Porfilio and Peter Scaglione have documented the "spatial lives" of the inhabitants of the Parkview Hotel, an SRO on Central Park North. Standards are under development from this material for actual designs.

At the same time, a studio investigation of the problem has occurred. The results are published in this and the last issue of *Precis*. In 1981, an added philosophical concern was introduced in the House of Thoreau sketch problem.

Most importantly, this program which is now a part of the newly formed Community Design Work-

shop, has led to real projects. Bob Lane and I have researched the neighborhood of Washington Heights with community representatives and the Coalition for the Homeless of New York City and have developed designs for a community residence which will be constructed in 1983.

I have been fortunate also to design a model apartment hotel for older people in Chelsea. The Vera Institute for Justice formulated the program and will manage the facilities. Construction will begin in the spring of 1983.

From the interdisciplinary Columbia University Community Services Project under the direction of Dr. Melvin Herman, to the work of the students at the Parkview Hotel and on the studio drawing boards, to the upcoming construction and the development of a permanent Community Design Workshop in the school, the years on this project have been exciting and productive. They form a link between the diverse professional schools, the development of a pedagogy, the refinement of a building type and a contribution to the community. I would like to thank my co-worker in studio, Michel Kagan, for his design sense and commitment to the urban program of the 20th century city.

[1]Thomas Butler Gunn, *The Physiology of New York Boarding Houses,* New York, 1857, p. 200.
[2]Gunther Barth, *City People,* New York, 1980, p. 42.
[3]Joan Hatch Shapiro, *Community of the Alone,* New York, 1971, p. 150.
[4]*Ibid.*

Esquisse: House of Thoreau
Critic: Michael Mostoller and
Michel Kagan
Second year, fall 1981

1. Colin Cathcart
2. and 3. Sheryl Kolasinski

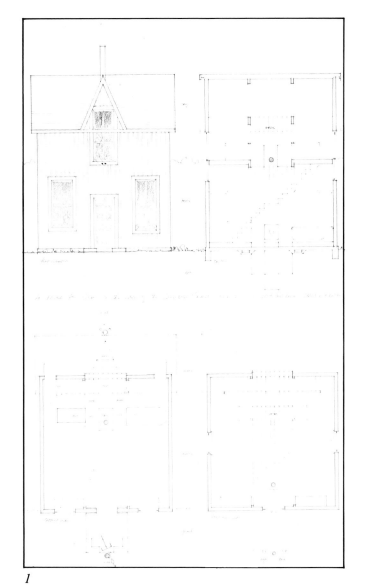

1

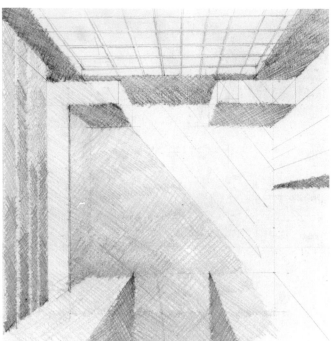

2

3

4. and 5. Derek Clarke
6., 7. and 8. John Loomis

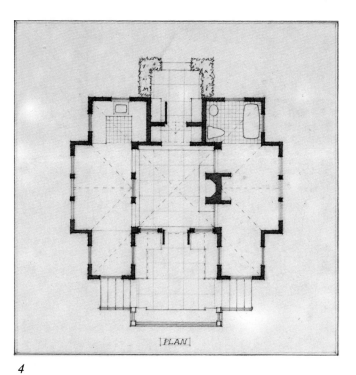

4

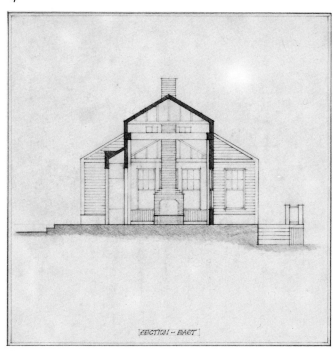

5

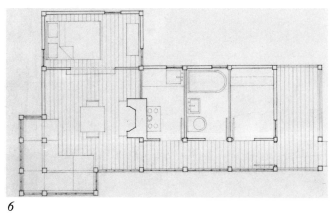

6

7

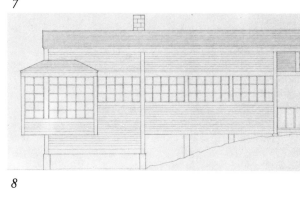

8

Single Room Occupancy
High-Rise Housing
Colin Cathcart and Keith Hone
Critics: Michael Mostoller and
Michel Kagan
Second year, fall 1981

1. Concept diagram
2. Tower elevation

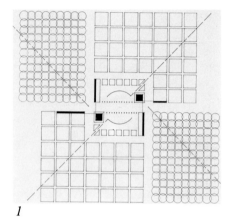

1

This "high rise housing with shared services" project is a specific response to two general concerns about American cities. The first is the accommodation of the single, unattached lifestyle of all income levels; the second, the urban scales of the street, the neighborhood, and the city as a whole.

A large, square (13 feet by 13 feet), well-lit room for each person is the premise for our project. The rooms are combined in various ways to permit a wide variety of dwellings and are ordered on the block according to common practice. Families have backyards; "rooming house" rooms are placed above the family units. Newcomers to the city and friends sharing apartments are housed in slabs which frame and overlook the parks.

The two towers mark the corners of Central Park and Morningside Park and have luxury loft spaces on their upper floors. Institutional and commercial uses line the more public streets, Central Park West and 110th Street. The lower buildings and the bases of the taller buildings relate formally and materially to the surrounding neighborhood, while the towers communicate with the entire city.

2

3. *110th Street perspective*
4. *Typical tower plan, SRO floor*
5. *SRO room perspective*
6. *Site, block and context
   block plans*
7. *Site axonometric*

3

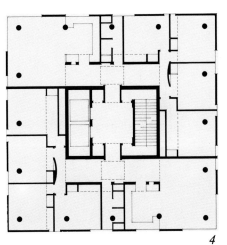

4

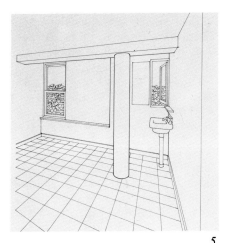

5

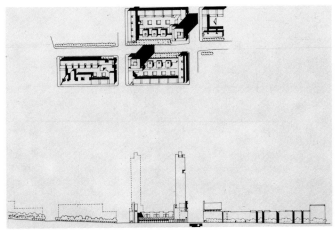

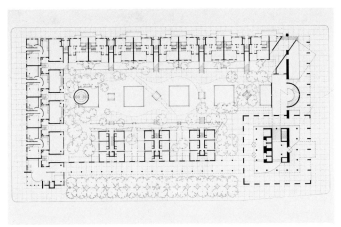

6

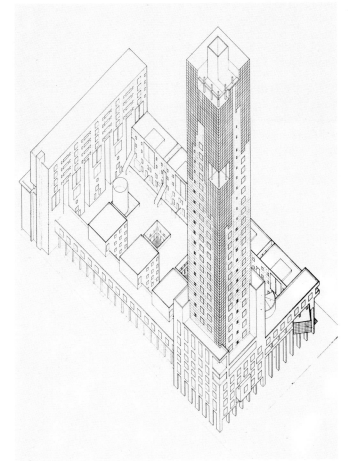

7

**Single Room Occupancy
High-Rise Housing
Kevin Dickey and John Loomis
Critics: Michael Mostoller and
Michel Kagan
Second year, fall 1981**

*1. Perspective from Central Park
2. Street level block plan*

The attempt to repair the urban fabric and context at Frederick Douglass Circle is inseparable from concentration of the social fabric. This project responds to the site urbanistically by restoring the townhouse scale street wall and marking the circle as a place with two towers. It responds to the community by providing a social service magnet to Harlem: a high school, library, performing arts center and gym on the northwest block. By placing this block at its core, the project acknowledges the ideals of Frederick Douglass. The towers and block of institutional services have a reciprocal relationship: whereas the towers frame Central Park, act as topographical anchors and imply a diagonal towards Morningside Park, the block is bounded by the parks.

The low-rise housing is designed for families. The tower is mixed use with commercial space, daycare and residents' facilities at the base. The upper stories contain half SRO housing for the elderly, half one bedroom apartments and lofts. The prismatic facades of the towers which face each other across the circle contain the office entrances and express the communal space for the SRO floors.

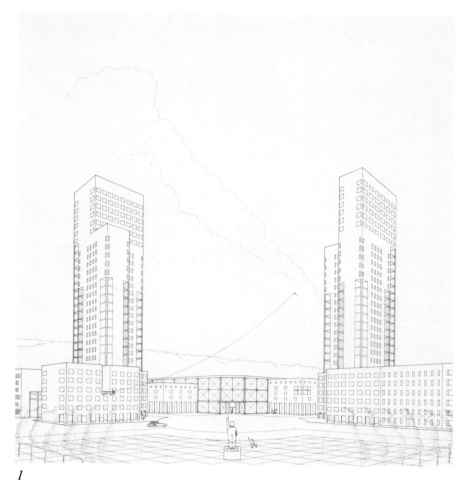

1

2

68

3. *Axonometric*
4. *Garden level block plan*
5. *Gallery level at tower*
6. *Typical upper floor*

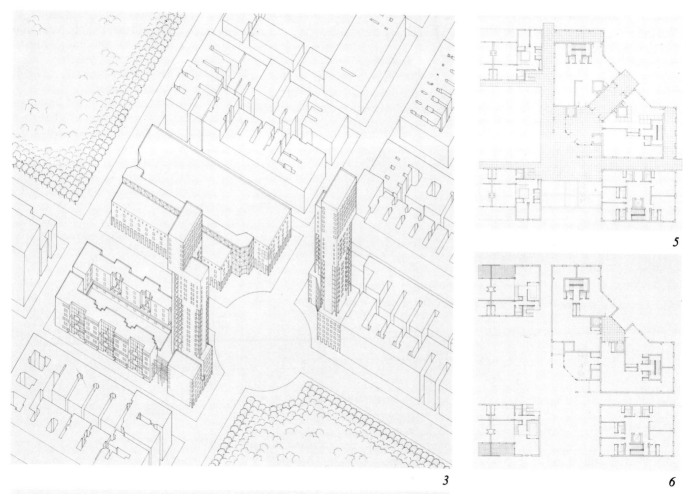

3

5

6

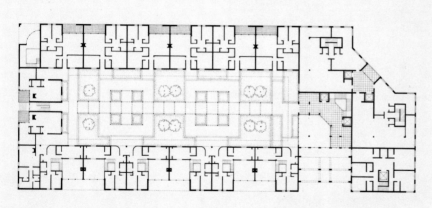

4

Museum Projects:
Master of Science
Building Design
Second Year Studio
Master of Architecture
Spring 1982

Whitney Museum Addition
New York, New York
Steven Peterson

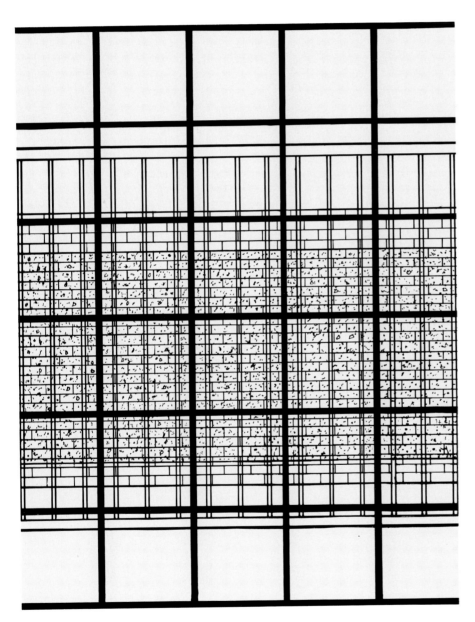

The project for an addition to the Whitney Museum of American Art is paradoxical: the building program requires growth, yet the composition of the existing building makes it formally unextendable.

Within the studio, two basic approaches were taken: the first and strategically simpler, was to make the addition a separate pavilion. The more difficult choice, which most students attempted, was to modify the existing building in relation to the addition in order to reflect a new unified form for the whole institution. The important issue for the studio, therefore, became that of completion, not addition, interaction, not competition.

Is a representation of the museum as a whole possible? Is the only recourse in the criticism of Marcel Breuer's original building in particular, and that of modernism in general, that we leave it alone as a preserved monument? The design work and class discussion addressed and reflected this controversy, with all of its implications for contemporary architecture.

Whitney Museum Addition
New York, New York
Robert A. M. Stern

National Museum of American Quilts
Washington, D.C.
Susana Torre

Barnett Newman Museum
New York, New York
Lauretta Vinciarelli

The project for an addition to the Whitney Museum of American Art was undertaken shortly after the Museum had hired Michael Graves as its architect and while the Museum's program was in a formative stage.

The inherently anti-contextual character of Marcel Breuer's original building rendered the task of designing an addition particularly daunting. The fact that, despite its now-questioned aesthetic premises, Breuer's building has become a potent symbol of the Museum propelled the studio's participants to consider the evolving conception of modernity in Modern Architecture and the American-ness of American art and architecture.

Studio discourse released a wide range of design responses, from "conservative" contextualism to "radical" classicism. Stylistic issues were viewed in plastic terms, leading to a consideration of exterior and interior architecture. In addition, the symbolic implications raised by a self-conscious investigation of "the styles" were tackled in relation to the problem of the art museum and architecture's responsibility to its own past.

The character of Manhattan's urbanism and the dialogue between container and contained that is fundamental to the museum type led the students towards an examination of streets, objects and rooms. The special character of the problem proved an effective provocation: the making of architecture once again functioned as a critical act.

This project for the only museum site still available on the Washington Mall (opposite I.M. Pei's East wing) was given to fulfill the requirements of the design curriculum and to explore issues of style and spatial organization.

American quilts, as an art form, provide powerful abstract interpretation of American buildings and landscapes. Patterns with names like Courthouse Steps, Barn Raising, Schoolhouse, Windmills were meant as representations of elements of the natural and built environments of the quilt makers. Sometimes, quilts represented specific landscapes (towns or private estates) or political statements, as in the underground railroad designs. Quilts are also useful, functional objects, making their status as art a matter of interpretation.

The challenge posed by this museum's design involves redefinition of spatial types and stylistic representation. For example, the esthetic of the quilts' patterns, creating multiple, simultaneous visual readings is different and seemingly opposite to the esthetic of traditional museums on the Mall, designed as interpretations of the classical style and its principles of order. By extension, the design of the display places became an investigation of the space of the American landscape. Most projects in the studio used grids, streets, classical "fronts" and modern "backs," ornament as an abstraction of nature and matrix-like spaces reminiscent of the composition of Kahn's museums. The reference to Kahn was not incidental; the possibility of continuing a flexible, open space within the virtual spatial definition of rooms was an objective in the studio. A modern interpretation of classical form became a parallel goal.

Besides the disciplinary "concrete", as Della Volpe would call the scientific side of architecture, "questioning" is the major objective of teaching. Questioning, during this term, meant to investigate the nature of a particular public institution: the museum. The choice of a museum for the permanent installation of the work of one artist seemed to me appropriate as a counterpart to the current idea of what a museum should be. Should museums be anthologies or should they provide the reading of an entire text? This question has deep implications for the notion of knowledge today. Too often knowledge is confused with information.

The choice of Barnett Newman's work is, to a certain extent, arbitrary; the work could have been Pollock's, for instance. Nevertheless to consider the work of an artist of the New York School was very intentional vis-a-vis the progressive disappearance of their work from New York.

A museum is a building whose use, in terms of what people do there, is very difficult to conceptualize. Very often the human performance is abridged in the notion of movement and museums are designed on flow patterns. I reversed the problem and I proposed a museum as the house of art, so that the building could have a clear specificity, geared to a definite collection of paintings.

Whitney Museum Addition
Terence M. Riley
Critics: Steven Peterson and
Charles Gwathmey
Master of Science, Building Design,
spring 1982

1. *Courtyard perspective*
2. *First and second floor axonometric*
3. *Fourth mezzanine and fifth floor axonometric*
4. *Exterior perspective*

1

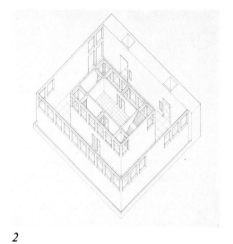

2

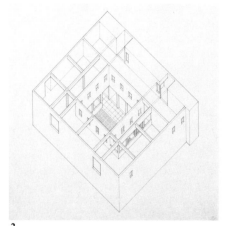

3

Central to the concept of a permanent collection is the notion that individual works of art acquire greater significance when viewed as part of a larger body of work. Accepting this, the curator's arrangement of the sequence of work is as significant as the pieces themselves.

Recognizing the importance of the permanent collection as a whole, as well as the sequence, this scheme proposes to organize the museum vertically. The existing Whitney becomes changing exhibit space, the addition housing the permanent collection. This organization is expressed as a formal transformation from a solid-in-a-void at street level to a void-in-a-solid at the top. This organization emphasizes the sequential nature of the collection and provides an appropriate beginning (pavilion in a double height space) and end (skylit courtyard) to that sequence.

The head of Apollo, the god of the arts, symbolically represents all the works of art in the museum. It also represents the idea that by viewing the collection, an isolated visual experience can be transformed into an intellectual one.

4

1. Interior perspective
2. Fifth floor plan
3. Exterior perspective

Whitney Museum Addition
William J. MacDonald
Critics: Steven Peterson and
Charles Gwathmey
Master of Science, Building Design,
spring 1982

1

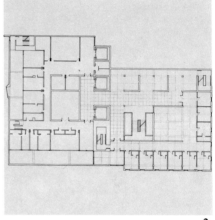

2

The addition to the Whitney Museum establishes a dialectic relationship with the existing building while responding to formal and spatial constraints presented by the specific urban context. The project developed through a typological and morphological investigation of museums in an attempt to determine the next logical step in the transformation and progression of the museum as a building type.

The existing building, which houses changing exhibitions, and the addition, containing the permanent collection, are organized around a court and vertical circulation system which is utilized as an orientation device for the horizontal and vertical procession through the new building.

The strategy was to enhance the ideas and principles of the existing building by reinterpreting them to derive and define the addition.

3

Whitney Museum Addition
Kathryn Dethier
Critics: Steven Peterson and
Charles Gwathmey
Master of Science,
Building Design, spring 1982

1. First floor plan
2. Second floor plan
3. Madison Ave. elevation
4. 75th Street elevation
5. Interior perspective

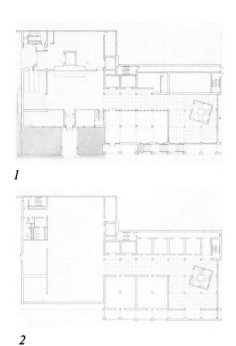

1

2

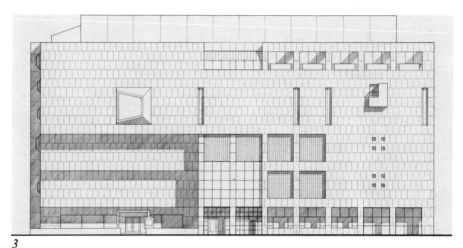

3

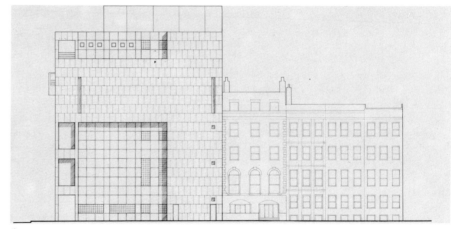

4

In adding to Marcel Breuer's Whitney Museum of Art, one confronts changing notions of architectural space and the viewing of art. Because the addition houses the permanent collection of art which ranges from small prints to the environmental art of the sixties, this project attempts to combine both the free plan of the Whitney with a more contemporary notion of discrete rooms. A gallery flanked with rooms of varying sizes terminates in a square loft space. A rotated stair within the loft space serves as a constant point of reference.

The implicit layering of Breuer's stepped facade is made explicit by the thick wall of the addition which reasserts the street wall. The addition is integrated into a unified facade through a series of recentering devices.

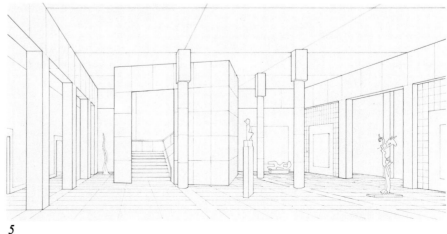

5

1. *Madison Ave. elevation*
2. *First floor plan*
3. *Site plan*
4. *Interior perspective*

Whitney Museum Addition
James Borchard
Critics: Steven Peterson and
Charles Gwathmey
Master of Science,
Building Design, spring 1982

The addition of permanent gallery space to the Whitney provides the opportunity to explore the architectural implications of changing attitudes toward viewing art. The present Whitney loft spaces will house temporary exhibits. The addition of a system of discrete rooms for the permanent collection establishes a dialogue between the existing Whitney and the addition in terms of closed/open, frontality/rotation, and center/periphery.

The exterior expression makes one museum of two equal cubic volumes, one stepped, the other rotated. A 'frame' for the gallery spaces in the addition is created on the exterior by extending part of the Whitney's facade. The structural frame is used to express the galleries within this frame and to address various scales: those of the street, the avenue, as well as the existing Whitney.

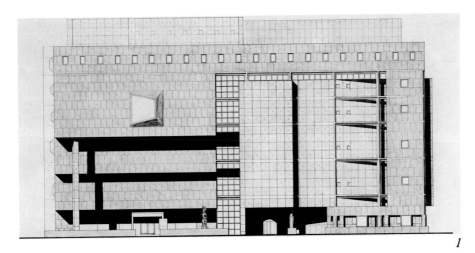

1

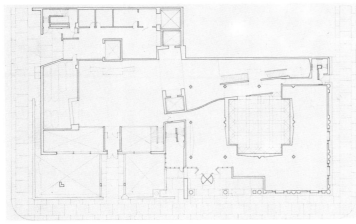

2

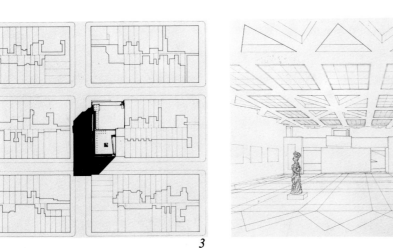

3

4

Whitney Museum Addition
Graham S. Wyatt
Harry H. Toung
Critic: Robert A. M. Stern
Second year, spring 1982

1. *Wyatt: Interior perspective*
2. *Wyatt: Fifth floor plan*
3. *Toung: Section*
4. *Toung: Exterior perspective*

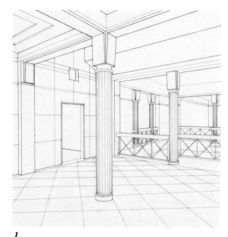

1

Wyatt: The nine bay structural system accommodates gallery space for the collection of pre-twentieth century art. A mezzanine of office space is inserted along the second, third and fourth floors. The top floor contains a series of skylit galleries surrounding an interior courtyard, which brings light to the fourth floor.

Toung: The exterior volume seeks to reestablish the classical tripartite tradition. A small pavilion containing additional restaurant seating defines street lines, centers the existing entrance and weaves together the old and new.

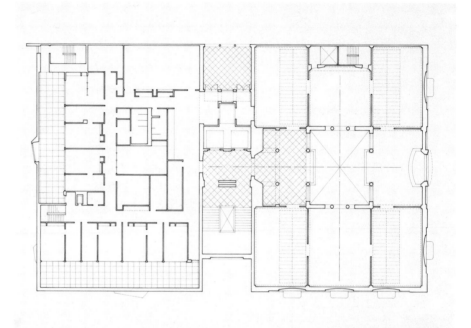

2

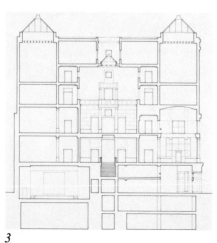

3

4

1. Longitudinal section
2. Madison Avenue elevation

Whitney Museum Addition
Richard K. Levitz
Critic: Robert A. M. Stern
Second year, spring 1982

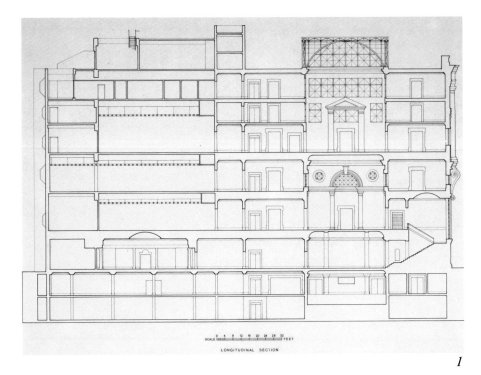

LONGITUDINAL SECTION

1

This solution is based on two attitudes with respect to the Museum type: the use of well-defined, figural rooms, in contrast to the loft space of the existing Whitney; and, treatment of the building as a treasure chest, as an expression of its contents, in contrast to the minimalist, sculptural qualities of the existing Whitney.

Through the juxtaposition and alignment of classical elements with the stepping facade, the existing Whitney, virtually scaleless, becomes more understandable. Though over-scaled and, perhaps, distorted here, the classical language retains its representational qualities. The humanizing effect of this language is sought through the attention given to various scale readings: a base of shops relates to the pedestrian scale, which is reiterated by the crown of figures at the roofline; lower orders relate to the subdivisions of the interior; giant orders relate to the city scale.

The duality which results from this solution provokes a dialogue between the old and new Whitney, between modernity and tradition—a continuing dilemma in the arts.

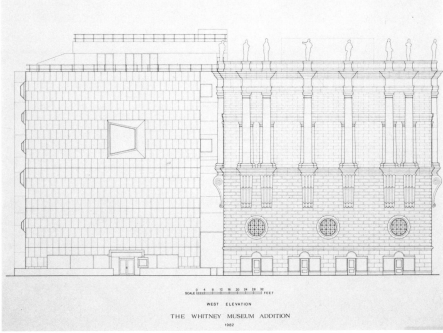

WEST ELEVATION
THE WHITNEY MUSEUM ADDITION
1982

2

National Quilt Museum
Washington, D.C.
Keith Hone
Critic: Susana Torre
Second year, spring 1982

1. Site plan
2. Section
3. Gallery perspectives
4. Main floor plan

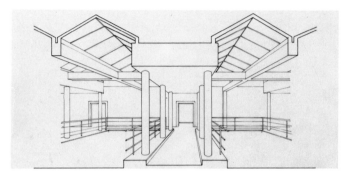

1

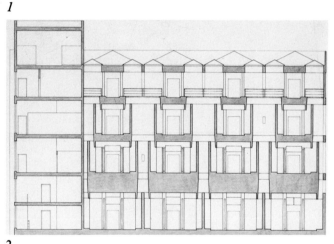

2

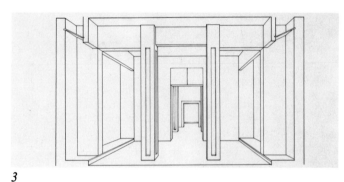

3

The spatial, processional and symbolic aspects of the Museum are specific to the dimensions and theme —the American landscape—of the quilts it is to house. The dimensions and proportions of the grid are based on the quilts. Layers parallel to the Mall and three major verticals establish a hierarchy of places for the individual, nature and society. The center court is a metaphor for the American landscape (generated from Jefferson's National Survey); the east room with its view of the Capitol is the place of the collective; the west tableaux rooms are the places of the individual.

The stepped section provides natural down-lighting for each quilt to accent its qualities as low-relief sculpture and to comment on the cultural vision that considers functional objects as art.

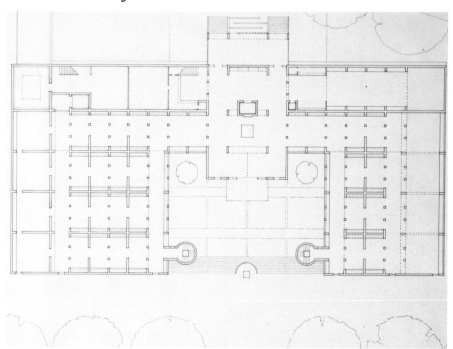

4

1. *First and third plans*
2. *Second and fourth plans*
3. *Mall elevation*
4. *Section*

National Quilt Museum
Washington, D.C.
Randy Correll
Critic: Susana Torre
Second year, spring 1982

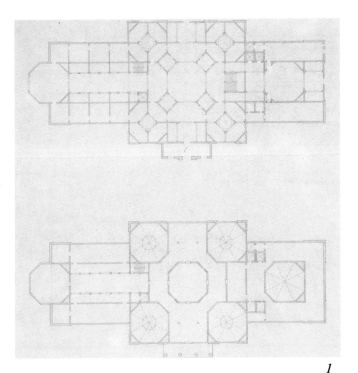

1

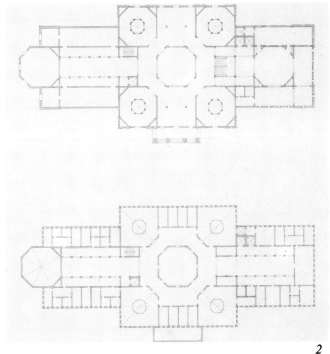

2

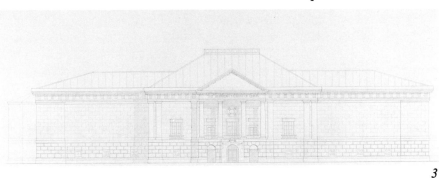

3

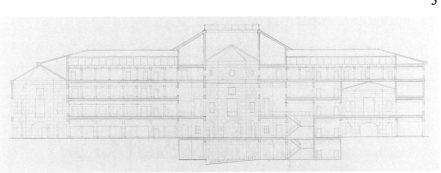

4

This project is an exploration of American classical architecture and the use of pattern as planar and spatial generator. The central and west wing contain the public galleries; the east wing the supporting services.

The small, sequential galleries on the first floor familiarize the visitor with the making, classification and cultural genre of quilts. The large octagonal volumes on the second floor provide a kaleidoscopic overview of the treasures of the collection. The smaller gallery spaces on the second and third floors of the west wing are for special exhibits. The fourth floor contains administrative and curatorial offices and study areas which are hidden behind the exterior frieze (the triglyphs of which are windows).

The facade is a personal exploration of grammar and syntax of classical architecture.

**Museum for the Work of
Barnett Newman**
Peter Wiles
Critic: Lauretta Vinciarelli
Second year, spring 1982

1. Gallery axonometric
2. Ground level plan

The program for this project was to design a permanent home for Barnett Newman's life work: over one hundred paintings and several pieces of sculpture. This design reflects an attitude toward Newman's art and the principles and spirit of the artist himself. As Newman had devoted himself to inspiring other young American artists, his museum will do the same by providing artist loft spaces, street galleries and shops. A small art library, lecture hall and visiting artists' exhibition space would invite public interest and participation.

Since Newman's work is best seen as a sequential continuum, this design encourages chronological viewing. The basic organizing element is a courtyard with a second story gallery encircling it. At ground level and accessible from the street are the loft spaces and shops. The museum proper is on the second level, accessible from the gallery. The directional arrangement encourages, but does not require, one to move sequentially past Newman's paintings, with the exception of the large, semi-circular space in which the fourteen "Stations of the Cross" are exhibited.

The visitor is always aware of his progress and orientation since his path intermittently returns to the courtyard space. He experiences the *oeuvre complete* through the closed, circular system. He recognizes that there is a beginning and an end, not a mysterious maze, and that, above all, this is a museum dedicated to a single artist.

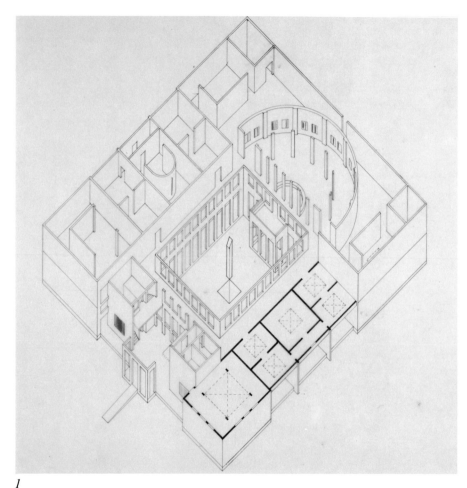

1

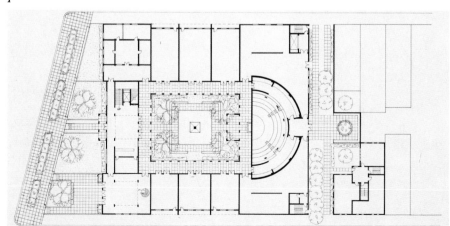

2

1. *Spring Street perspective*
2. *Interior perspective*
3. *Ground level plan*
4. *Section*

**Museum for the Work of
Barnett Newman
Colin Cathcart
Critic: Lauretta Vinciarelli
Second year, spring 1982**

1

2

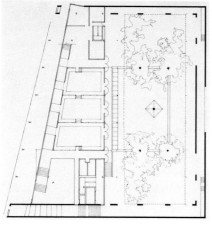

3

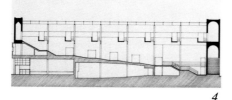

4

2. to interpret the material qualities of the neighborhood (cast iron, fire-escapes, brick and plaster), its urban structure (warped grid and lot lines), and its activities (dwellings, workshops, and stores) without mimicking the forms of nearby buildings.

3. to make a secretly classical building cut with limitless American spaces.

Three intentions guided the design of this museum:

1. to give a psychological impression of the life of an American artist by means of an architectural promenade which reinforces the contemplation of his work;

On Museums
Colin Cathcart

The design of a museum is among the most subtle problems in architecture, resisting straightforward categorization. For example, it is an undeniably "public" place, but it is also a setting for the personal (and thus "private") encounter with art. The nature of the museum as a design problem can be approximated by a series of critical analogies with other building types. Though no one museum is exclusively a "palace for art", or a "department store of art", or a "treasury vault for art", there is a grain of truth in each analogy.

The form of the traditional museum was generated in a discourse between *the palace* and *the studio,* between the place which commissions art and the place which creates it. Even in populist America, the sense of pomp and ceremony which pervades museum architecture confirms the high cultural status of art patronage. On the other hand, most art suffers when it is placed in anything but a relatively humble, well-lit room. Thus, the familiar hierarchy is established, from the grand cour d'honneur, the broad steps, the portico and the rotunda, to the comfortably proportioned rooms which accommodate the art itself.

The masters of the modern movement, critical of typological tradition and representation, proposed highly conceptual and experimental museum visions. Something was lost and something was gained, but in the process the art community turned away from architecture. Conventional wisdom now insists that architecture "distracts" from art. In response, many contemporary art museums are akin to "non-architectural" building types: *the convention center, the shopping mall, the department store.* In the first analogy, the museum is seen as an empty vessel, a well-served shed, the interior of which is reconstructed with each new exhibition. In the second analogy, architecture is separated from the art and confined to areas of pure circulation. The display areas are considered simply as bulk space, where episodic installations and reams of public relations hype threaten to reduce museum going to a form of shopping. Centre Pompidou may serve as a double illustration. It is a convention center, a mechanical and structural celebration of enclosure, and it is also a shopping mall, with undifferentiated display spaces strung out along its one truly architectural element, the escalator. In the case of the Whitney Museum, the monumental exterior cloaks a six story department store. Architecture does not conflict with art, but the permanence of architecture can only obstruct the transience and commercialism implied by modern curatorial practice.

There are two analogous building types which speak to the positive role architecture can play in relating art to the modern city: *the sanctuary* and *the train station.* The museum is a sanctuary because it is an alternative to the public realm, not merely its indoor extension. The more active and transient our cities become, the greater the need is to stabilize our culture in a special, quiet place where time is permitted to stand still. Like the eye of a hurricane, the museum is a place of reflective silence in the midst of the non-stop modern city, a sanctuary in a vortex of time and space.

Simultaneously, the museum must provide a gateway between these two opposing realms. Many old train stations provide just such a gateway, heightening the city dweller's anticipation of travel, and then monumentally welcoming the traveller back to the city. By dramatizing the juncture between the city and the realm of art, the architecture of the museum can honor both. The new East Wing of the National Gallery is a marvelous train station without being a good sanctuary. The great atrium heightens one's psychological awareness of art, but leads to gallery spaces which are mean and cramped. A good modern museum must be both a sacred preserve of art and a gateway to this preserve from the surrounding city, expressing correspondence and allowing each realm to beckon to the other.

Other building type analogies suggest themselves: a library for storing the knowledge of art, a school for learning about art, a treasury for valuable art, a mausoleum for dead art. The British Art Museum at Yale shares in the analogies discussed above, each in its proper place and proportion. It is both a palazzo and an aggregate of small rooms, a hierarchical system and a maze. There is a clear separation between permanence and transience; a three dimensional concrete grid is elevated as a *piano nobile* above rented commercial spaces.

Unlike most fields of human action, an architectural act is permanent. The museum buildings of Kahn, Aalto, Soane, Schinkel and Von Klenze still stand in our world today. The architectural achievements of the past exist in the present as a concrete standard against which current building can be judged. The museum designs included in this issue of *Precis* reaffirm the role of museum architecture as a spatial expression of art and as a response to the city, but most clearly respond to this silent critique of history.

**Second Year Studio
Master of Architecture
Spring 1982**

**Community Center for the
Salvation Army
Spring Valley, New York
Steven Holl**

**Community Church of New York
Development
New York, New York
Timothy Wood**

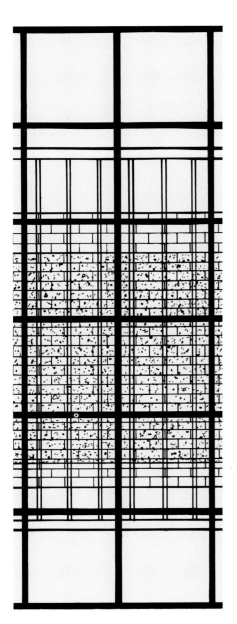

What is architecture and what is merely building construction? In the project for a 12,000 square foot Community Center for the Salvation Army, the economy of means necessitated by the institution's finances helped bring this question into focus. Each gesture was considered in light of this condition. The materials and construction, as well as an overall idea of what makes the whole greater than the sum of the parts, were stressed.

General issues addressed in the studio were:

1) the relation of the new structure to the existing pattern of the town;

2) the history of the site;

3) existing and historically comparable building types;

4) the relationship between building and grounds;

5) clarity of architectural concepts;

6) proportion;

7) light; and

8) the relationship of details to mass.

The program was written by the Salvation Army.

The Community Church of New York development project was adopted because, in addition to conforming to the studio's requirement for a cultural or institutional building, it offered the opportunity to work with an actual site and client while addressing current issues in urban architecture.

Programmatically, the project involved the expansion and renovation of the existing church and church-sponsored facilities and the design of a major speculative highrise on the church's valuable midtown site. The program consisted of spaces for religious ritual, social gathering, education, administration and miscellaneous community activities as well as the tower's parking, large scale vertical circulation and mechanical and structural systems.

Pedagogically, establishing the programmatic framework in terms of client needs and aspirations and city zoning and massing criteria became the initial "design undertaking." Since "program" was not pre-defined, the potential of the site and client goals made it possible to adopt different strategies and, thus, define the program specifically in terms of their architectural resolution.

The fundamental normal problems posed by the project were the insertion of a mid-block tower into a context of mixed high and low-rise buildings; the creation of a "base" structure serving the church spaces; the relationship of the new building ensemble to both a residential side street and a major commercial cross street; and the sorting out of a myriad of functional, contextual and symbolic relationships.

Community Church of New York
Development
Alex Lamis
Critic: Timothy Wood
Second year, spring 1982

1. 34th Street elevation
2. Detail of 35th Street elevation
3. First floor plan

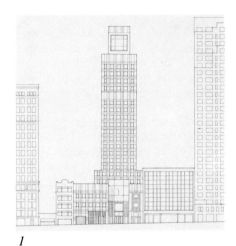

1

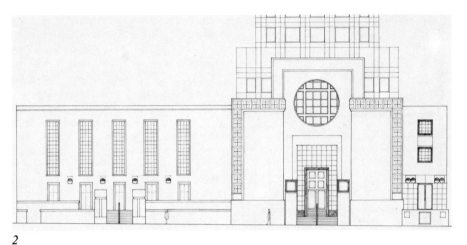

2

I felt that the expanded Unitarian Church must provide places for both private worship and public discussion. A new chapel, placed in the center of the block, is raised and removed from the street. Light floods the chapel from all sides. The existing worship hall has been recast as a forum, carrying forward the Unitarian's interest in secular issues.

I chose to develop the 34th Street side of the site as an office building. This development would allow the church to fund an expanded library, offices for non-profit organizations and other civic-minded programs.

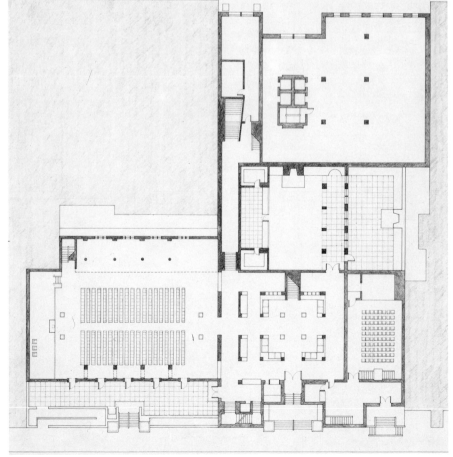

3

1. First floor plan
2. North-south section
3. 35th Street elevation

Community Church of New York Development
Dale Peterson
Critic: Timothy Wood
Second year, spring 1982

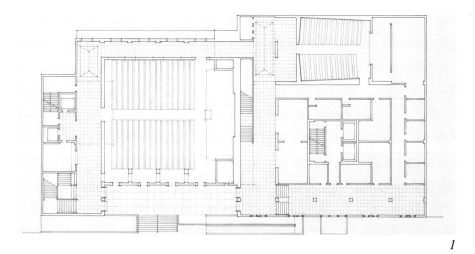

1

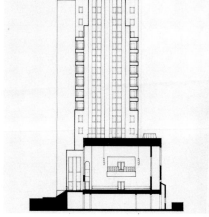

2

The solution proposed here derives its overall form from two considerations: a desire to make this development part of a whole-block composition and the need to preserve the institutional identity of the church in a large scale development which threatens to overwhelm it. The original church building has been kept and two new buildings have been added: a narrow tower of church offices and parsonages to the left of the church building and a large for-profit housing tower to the right (which also contains some community functions in its base).

The block has been changed from the typical Manhattan block with larger buildings at the end and smaller scale elements in mid-block. The pattern is reversed here with a new large-scale piece in the center and two minor small scale centers to either side: one the church and the other a pair of nineteenth century rowhouses preserved as a set-piece fragment of the block's earlier form. The block thus retains fragments from different stages in its evolution while being carefully composed to be a new and balanced composition.

3

**Community Center for the
Salvation Army
Spring Valley, New York
David DeValeria
Critic: Steven Holl
Second year, spring 1982**

*1. East-west section
2. Site plan
3. Axonometric*

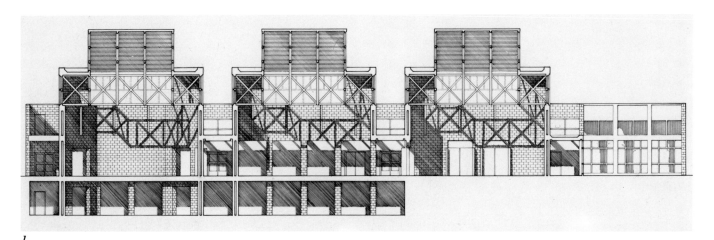

1

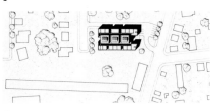

2

The Salvation Army has a history of using "found objects" for corps community centers. These buildings have been chosen more for their convenience and flexibility than for their appropriateness as evangelical settings. The reconciliation of the need for community service space with sectarian influence forms the theme for this building.

In keeping with the community center type, a flexible arrangement of regularized spaces is provided for classrooms, offices, etc. These ancillary spaces surround and inform the primary spaces of the chapel, auditorium and dining hall. The spaces are structured similarly throughout and natural lighting is employed in their characterization. The unification of the rational plan with a basilical section reinforces the major theme.

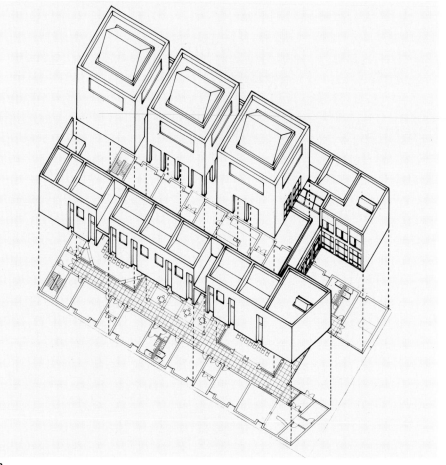

3

1. *London: First floor plan*
2. *London: Section*
3. *Szto: Axonometrics*

**Community Center for the
Salvation Army
Spring Valley, New York
Gabrielle London
John Szto
Critic: Steven Holl
Second year, spring 1982**

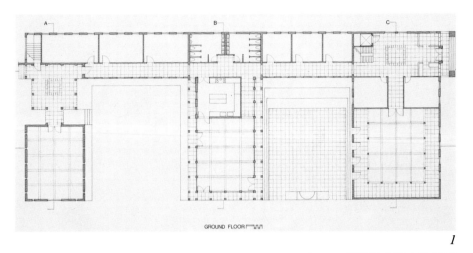

GROUND FLOOR

1

SECTION D

2

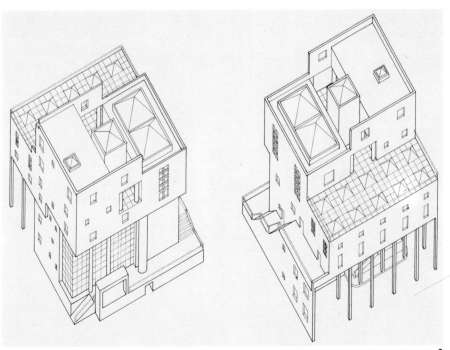

London: In this design the site was divided lengthwise into three parts. The program was then placed in the three areas of the site: the support services on the northern edge, the social gathering spaces in the central zone and the existing trees remained in the Southern band.

The support services were articulated as a narrow bar building which, with the open, tree area, serves as a backdrop for the gathering spaces. The meeting room, dining room and chapel were each placed in separate, pitched roofed volumes. The degree of openness, structural system and location of these volumes differentiate uses. The most public place, the meeting room, is in the most "urban" part of the site and is the most dense volume. The most private place, the chapel, is the most remote from Main Street and the most open volume.

Szto: Just north of New York City, Spring Valley serves as a community of safe harbor, assimilating many incoming families in their flight from the problems of urban life. The Salvation Army, in keeping with its philosophy of "soup, soap and salvation" has sculpted a program to deal with the special needs of this community.

Budget restraints guarantee an economy of structure. To comply with this primary consideration, a cubic volume is used as the container for the various parts of the program. Within the cube, architectural space and matter are organized using the principles of tension (dissonance) and resolution (harmony). The combination of these precepts creates an architecture in which ambiguity and asymmetry are resolved in a geometry based on the golden section.

3

Third Year Studio
Master of Architecture
Fall 1981

Luxury Hotel Development
New York, New York
Harold Fredenburgh

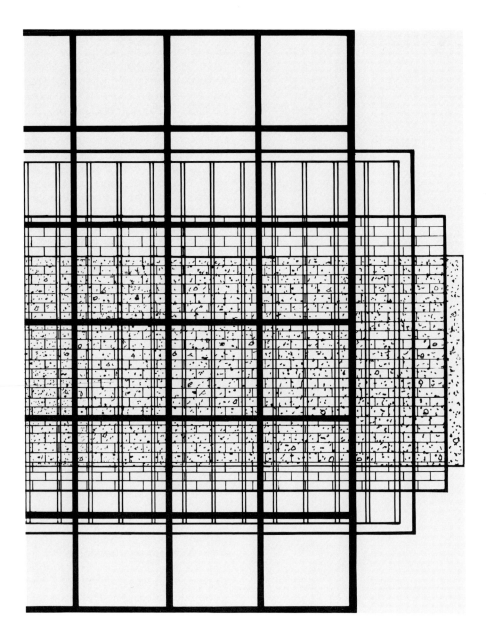

The city is an agglomeration of solutions to problems, and its fabric has been shaped and altered by large scale building. In a time when new public institutions (city governments, museums, libraries) present few opportunities for urban intervention, architects must understand the potential inherent in the "developer city." The hotel, a quasi-public building and a small city in itself, can act as a catalyst for the development of a district. In this studio, the hotel was seen as a building type which, from an urban design viewpoint, can move beyond its front door to support the richness of the urban fabric.

The site selected for this project is unique in Manhattan: 47th Street was to be widened from Fifth Avenue to the United Nations, giving that complex a proper gateway. Only the block between First and Second Avenue has, in fact, been widened, producing Dag Hammarskjold Plaza. The site, which includes a number of nearby developable parcels, combines a sense of place and outlook. The site and program together are of a size and structure which encourages an effective dialogue between planning and architecture.

Mixed-Use Complex
New York, New York
Ada Karmi-Melamede

Lincoln West Development
New York, New York
Alex Kouzmanoff

Conditions within the American building tradition at the end of the 19th century, including the availability of privately owned land and private capital, fostered inventive "mixed-use" proposals. Concurrently, new technological developments in structural framing, in mechanical movement systems, and later in mechanical environmental controls, allowed for the enclosure of unprecedented areas of the urban fabric. These early experiments have provided some cities with the wonderful places that have functioned like public "living rooms."

Recent "mixed-use" domains have, however, lost their "magic." They have been reduced to assemblages of isolated parts disposed according to zoning regulations and economic constraints. Whether as "atriums", "galleries", or "covered plaza", they fail to provide the connecting elements to the city fabric. They have become insulated and introverted spaces, adding more "self-sufficient" buildings to the city and greatly diminishing the urban experience.

The intent of the studio is to look into the nature of the "mixed-use" domains in light of previous American precedents and pursue two major issues inherent in these domains: 1) the relation of functional programmatic parts to a "conceptual whole;" and 2) the implication of the "whole" within and as a fragment of the city.

The following aspects structured this search:

1) Internal Hierarchy—between private and public

2) External Hierarchy—between object and context

3) Building Components' Transformation—constant vs. variables

4) Formal Expression—collective image vs. individual expression

"Mixed-Use" domains are evolving urban situations and not building types. In light of existing land use, where "single-use" zones prevail, the loss of these meeting places is detrimental to the urban balance.

Urbanization is a complex system of composite forces, a manifestation of natural phenomena, harmoniously linked to human wishes and desires, that is sensitive to "the multiple aspects of the complexity that constitutes each architectural work." For urbanization to succeed, it must possess the quality of being urbane—"civil and courteous." This is hardly the tenor of the times; nevertheless, architecture must be a part of a process that inspires hope, aspiration and intellectual pursuit as a counterforce to decay, despair and abandonment. So, more than theory clothed in the vagaries of "schematic mental games" and historical abstractions, the task is one of searching out themes commensurate with our perceptions of the city without inhibiting our minds and imagination from understanding the essence and dynamics of a city's continuum.

The quest to understand and evaluate the nature of the project to be built on this unique and abandoned parcel of land was paramount to the urban and architectural resolution. The proposals had to reflect certain "lines of force" which would bring into focus the tension created by the orthogonal grid of the city superimposed on the site, terminating in the Hudson River edge. Understanding this tension from a geographic and topographic sense was the challenge and the essence of the solutions. They are not to be considered as finished designs, but as catalysts for new ideas for the development of an urban place for recreation, living and working. This urban place exists within the context of a new environment in which man can find himself in his own dimensions in a past-future time frame.

Luxury Hotel Development
Elaine Felhandler
Critic: Harold Fredenburgh
Third year, fall 1981

1. Site axonometric
2. Site plan

The goal of this project is to create an urban precinct. The strategy for creating a precinct with a sense of coherence evolves directly from the examples of Tudor City, Beekman Place, and Rockefeller Center. The demolition of the "soft" inner core of the site allows a north-south mid-block street to be inserted which connects the three blocks. Buildings with "hard" qualities, such as the church, Japan House, and large apartment blocks, were left due to their importance to the community.

Running through the site from avenue to avenue, between 46th and 47th Streets, is Dag Hammarskjold Plaza, a dark, unused strip park. This area is covered with a commercial atrium space. The park has been concentrated within the north corner of the block.

The location for the hotel, between 46th and 47th Streets and 1st and 2nd Avenues, was chosen for its proximity to the United Nations and its prominence within the development. It is the culmination of the mid-block street and is acknowledged within the building as an internal street. The "street" creates a clear internal organization. The functions on the west relate to the hotel and its guests; to the east are the more public functions: shops, restaurants, and access to the upper restaurant and ballroom.

The massing of the facade creates two separate readings: that of a tower marking the end of the street and that of a mid-block, party-wall building which steps back in unison with the surrounding office buildings. The tower is completed by the "temple" top, common to early New York skyscrapers, which unifies the composition and creates the romantic mood appropriate to the life in a Manhattan hotel.

1

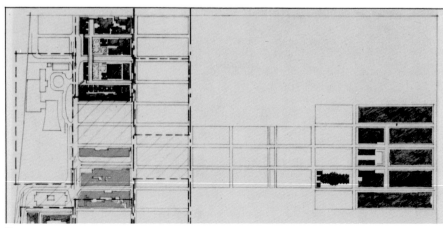
2

3. Hotel facade
4. Hotel section
5. Lobby level plan
6. 26th floor plan
7. Top floor perspective

3

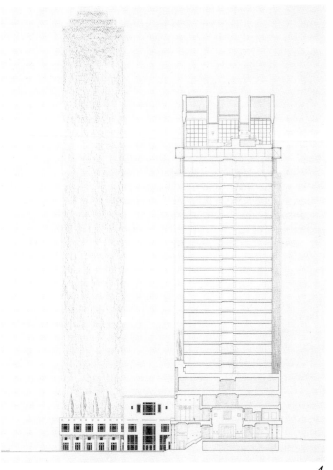

4

5

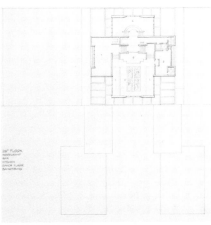

6

7

Luxury Hotel Development
Robert Burton
Critic: Harold Fredenburgh
Third year, fall 1981

1. First floor plan
2. Second floor plan
3. Typical hotel plan
4. Elevation
5. Section through lobby

Three Manhattan blocks adjacent to the United Nations are transformed into a dense urban center for New York's international community. The existing buildings are largely kept, as they are appropriate in scale and function for those thoroughfares. In the cleared interiors of the blocks, a series of tree-lined open spaces, pedestrian walks and arcades tie the blocks together north to south without effacing the city's street pattern. Low commercial pavilions partially fill the presently barren Dag Hammarskjold Plaza and connect the interior spaces to the avenues. Stepped-back slabs arranged around the new plazas provide office space for the many small consulates, national missions and international agencies scattered around the United Nations.

A new hotel acts as the architectural and social landmark of the new development. An entry square with a fountain and a series of lobbies leading to a cascading staircase give elements of processional drama to the events staged in the hotel's public rooms. While ground floor retail space and through-block arcades tie the hotel into the activity of the street, the ballroom, meeting rooms and main dining room all sit above and overlook the street and entry plaza. The pink granite and marble mass steps to a square midblock tower which faces the city in every direction. Beneath the gold leafed pyramidal roof, an intimate supper and dance club takes advantage of the nighttime views.

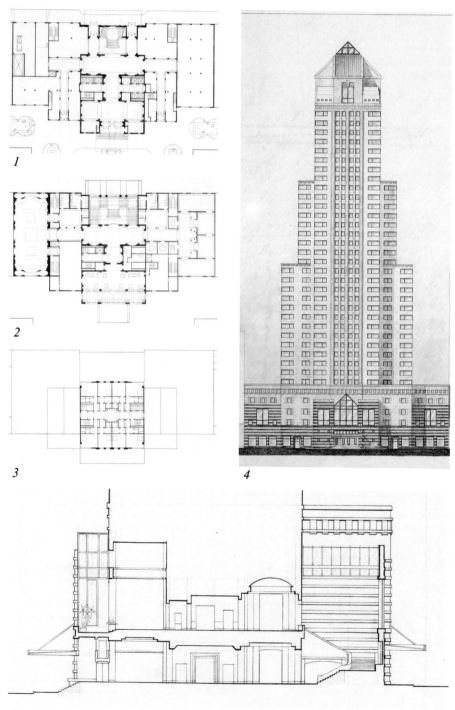

1

2

3

4

5

6. *Site axonometric*

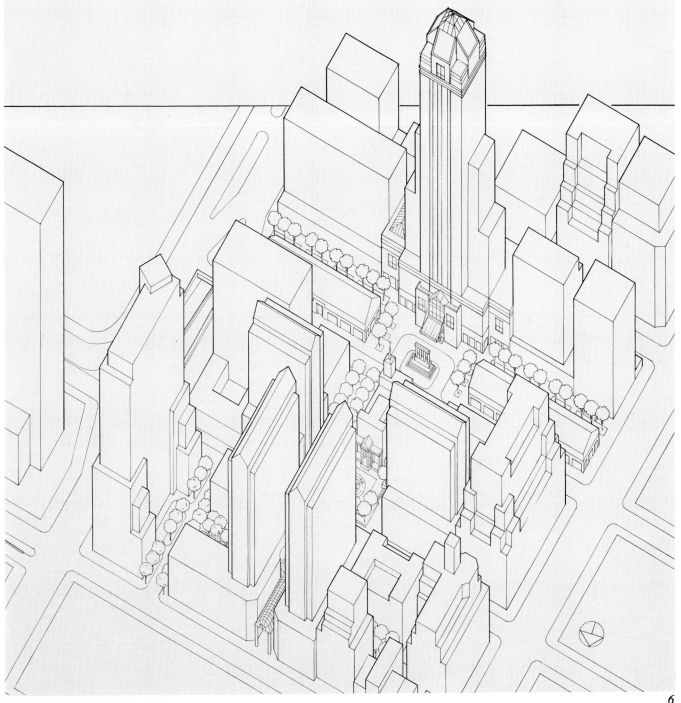

**Mixed-Use Complex: Christie's
Auction House
Neil McNulty
Critic: Ada Karmi-Melamede
Third year, fall 1981**

1. Perspective section
2. Perspective section

This project proposes both a strategy for dealing with the Manhattan waterfront and the creation of an urban event on the Upper East Side. Located on the two blocks that flank 72nd Street between York Avenue and the East River, it mediates between residential development to the north and institutions to the south.

The scheme incorporates:

1) a perimeter wall of housing which modifies the scale of the grid to give a conclusion at the water's edge.

2) a two-sided arcade with shops and offices in one half and auction rooms, display spaces and offices in the other. The seam of the arcade makes passage to the river the narrative of the design.

3) light industry, service and parking on the lower levels.

4) a park/promenade over F.D.R. Drive with a theater, restaurants and offices.

The first of the layers which focus on public space is a commercial piazza. It is a room of doors that serves as an entrance to the project as a whole and to the various elements of the layer beyond.

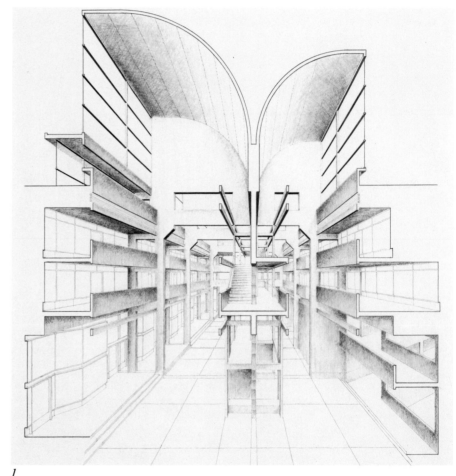

1

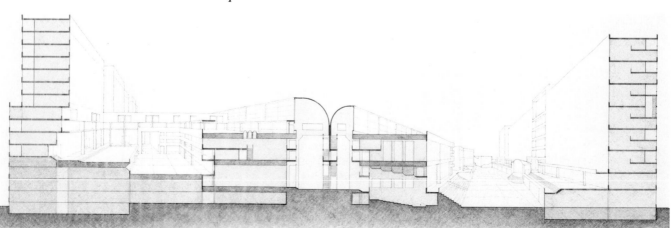

2

3. *Site axonometric*
4. *Courtyard level plan*
5. *Auction House level plan*

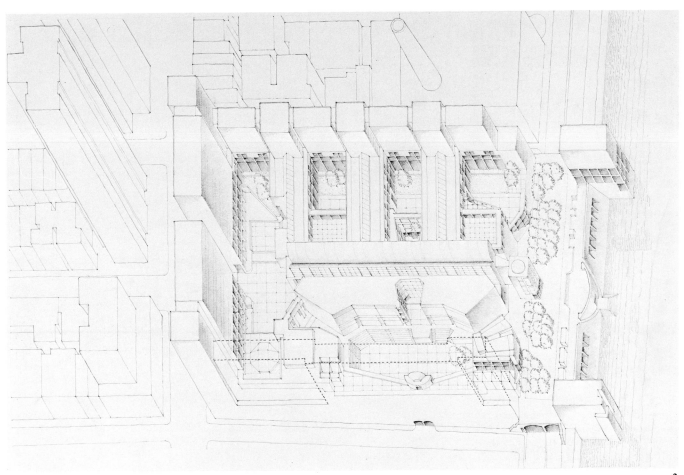

3

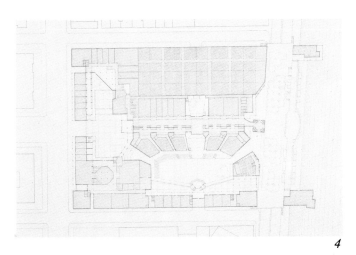

4

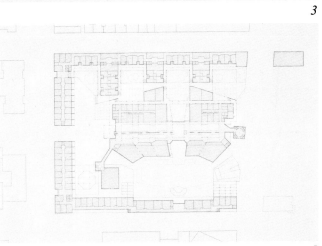

5

Lincoln West Development
John Reagan
Critic: Steven Peterson
Third year, fall 1981

1. *Existing site plan*
2. *Site plan*
3. *View from west*
4. *Detail of project area*

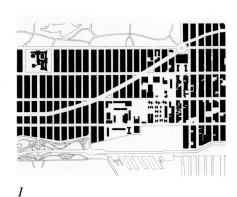

1

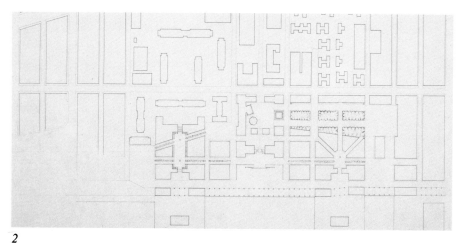

2

Traditionally, public spaces in New York City have turned inward with little direct relationship to the waterfront. Now that the pier warehouses and railyards are largely obsolete, the opportunity exists to re-examine the nature of the waterfront and to develop an urban center with a direct relationship to the waterfront.

The site for this exercise extends thirteen blocks along the Hudson River between 59th and 72nd Streets. It is the largest open parcel left in the city and its development is currently being studied.

In this scheme, the New York grid is extended into the site, but is distorted to create "double blocks" which terminate as large piers. The rhythm of single and double blocks create new circulation patterns and provide a transition in the street system as a way of ending the grid at the water's edge.

The hotel complex, a focus for the urban space, is linked to the waterfront by two sequences. First and more direct is a formal progression of stairs. The second is along a linear park, sloping and parallel to the river. The program pieces of the hotel are pulled apart and expressed as discrete objects which create a public square.

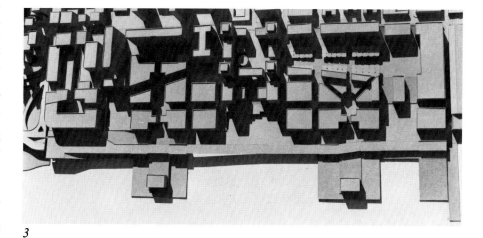

3

4

1. *Figure-ground plan*
2. *Site plan*
3. *View from northwest*
4. *Perspective of street*
5. *Perspective of court*

Lincoln West Development
Robert Lane
Critic: Steven Peterson
Third year, fall 1981

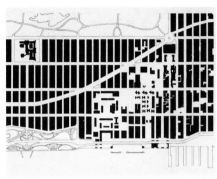

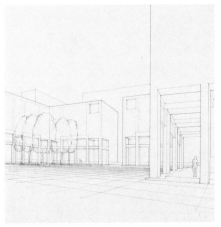

1

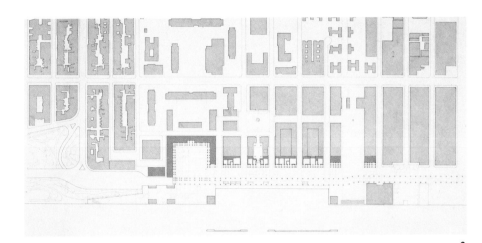

2

3

While it is true that there are distinct precincts and edges within the city, the continuity of the grid predominates. For this reason, the site was not treated as a set piece or single composition bounded by 11th Avenue. There is only one real edge to the project—the river and the highway that runs along it.

This solution attempts to intensify that edge and resolve as many of the connections of grid to edge as possible. These include the 60th Street connection to Columbus Circle, the potential connection to Lincoln Center and the crosstown bus route at 66th Street. Thus, the arcaded street and wall of high buildings serve as an organizing device for the site and for the largely disorganized fabric east of 11th Avenue. The street and wall terminate in a square building, an object building set against the housing slabs which extend beyond 11th Avenue.

4

5

Lincoln West Development
Kenneth Bainton
Critic: Alex Kouzmanoff
Third year, fall 1981

1. East-west section
2. North-south section
3. View from north
4. Detail of project area

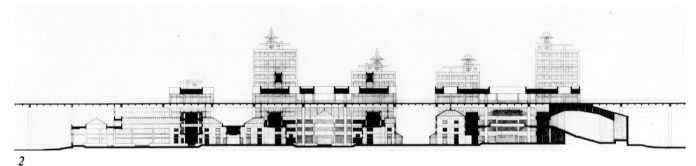

1

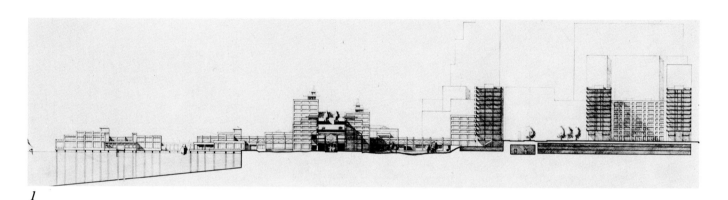

2

The major commercial concentration is located to the west of the three-block long rectangular public space near the center of the site. The 66th Street valley runs through this formal urban space and descends to the river's edge through a series of smaller, more informal, terracing spaces.

The nexus of public activity occurs at the intersection of these three blocks with the elevated West Side Highway which runs the length of the site. The highway is subsumed into the urban fabric by three buildings: the northern one houses theaters, the center an Olmstead museum and a multi-purpose hall, the southern a wintergarden.

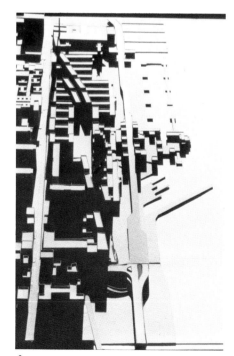

3

4

1. *Site plan*
2. *East-west section*
3. *Detail of project area*

Lincoln West Development
Thomas Brashares
Critic: Alex Kouzmanoff
Third year, fall 1981

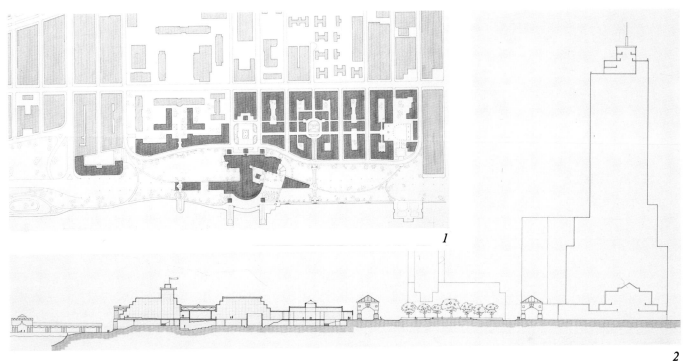

1

2

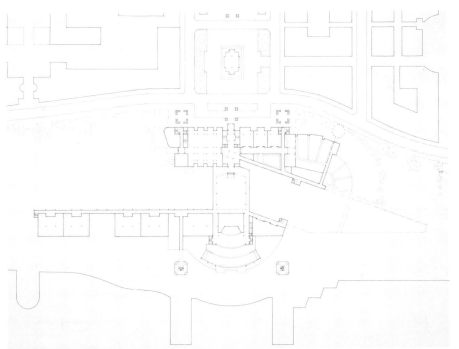

The continuation of Riverside Park and the character of Riverside Drive were the basic premises of my scheme. The project is tied together at an urban scale through the introduction of a curved loop road dividing the buildings from the park and by an east-west axis at 65th/66th Street.

At the end of this axis is the wintergarden, which becomes a gateway from the city to the river, with gatehouses as architectural symbols of this transition. The wintergarden, with its city room, Olmstead Museum, beer garden and commercial spaces, links the city plaza and the waterfront. An outdoor theater, waterfront walkway and recreational facilities under the highway are provided for neighborhood use and enjoyment.

3

**Third Year Studio
Master of Architecture
Spring 1982**

**Diplomatic Mission
New York, New York
Klaus Herdeg**

**Shakertown Visitors Center
Pleasant Hill, Kentucky
Michael Mostoller**

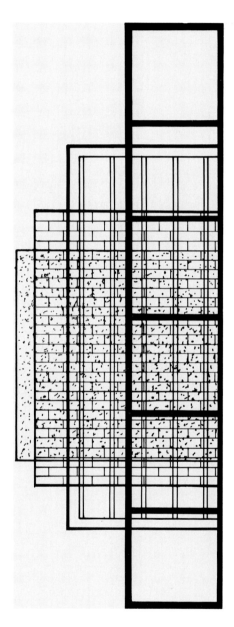

Quite unlike the usual procedure of analyzing a given program and a given site to induce, if not invent, a splendid product, this term-long problem was viewed as a means of exploring the full range of design opportunities. Ascertaining the "givens" was made part of the problem, thus requiring interaction among the students and with their critic in a form not unlike a seminar.

Given the general purpose of the building with a generic structure of program and site, the particulars had to be worked out collectively. Although it was stated that the building would house a mission to the United Nations and a consulate, with the proviso that the staff would be offered housing on the same site, the country to be represented still had to be decided. Weighing the pragmatic and symbolic implications, the students eventually agreed on Spain. While believing at the time of heated debate that this was going to be their crucial decision, many later discovered that they would have had the same struggles in organizing the same architectural elements in any country's diplomatic mission.

The location and size of a corner of a Manhattan block site was also decided by the group.

The details of the program were borrowed from two actual programs of much greater complexity. The site covers 12,000 square feet, the mission and consulate comprise about 30,000 sq. ft. and the residences 40,000 sq. ft. The latter includes lavish apartments for the chief delegate to the U.N., the consul general and a suite for state guests as well as thirty-one 1 to 3 bedroom apartments.

The three projects shown adhere closely to the program and site decisions made by the group.

The Shakers, during the 1800's, developed a highly successful experimental culture. This inspired group of religious zealots, simple and resourceful, has left a rich Shaker legacy in its architecture, environment and design.

A singularly innovative group, the Shakers held societal principles foreign to the nineteenth century but familiar to the twentieth. In advocating equality of the sexes, communal (if celibate) living, environmental conservation, pacifism and a philosophy of maximum utility in all things, the Shaker society was a unique phenomenon in its own time and a remarkable foreshadowing of ours.

Although there remain a few aged members of the Shaker sect, the experiment is finished. Now our look at the Shakers can only be retrospective through the remaining communities and through the rich heritage of Shaker design, architecture and philosophy.

The Visitors Center for the restored 19th century Shaker Village in Pleasant Hill, Kentucky was selected as a design problem because of three factors:

1. It was modest in scale. This allowed for comprehensive and complete development.

2. It had to fit into an already intricately ordered context of contours, forms, building types, spatial order and materials.

3. It confronted the students with the Shaker's extraordinary, articulate attitudes towards the act of making objects and buildings.

The program goals include restoration of the original buildings to their historic use and relocation of some of the exhibits and activities to a new facility.

Community for 5000 Inhabitants, Cuba
Fernando Salinas, Roberto Segre (visiting critics from the University of Havana, Cuba) and Michel Kagan

The Visitors Center should provide exhibition space for those items presently owned but not housed at Shakertown including clothing, rugs and rare books.

To intensify the public educational experience, a general history of the Shakers' life and customs from the beginning of the movement in England to the arrival of the first Shakers at Pleasant Hill should be presented.

Emphasis should be given to the singular qualities of Shaker life. Their faith was important in all phases of their life. The spirit and precepts embodied in the art of the Shakers, their furniture and artifacts, pertain to time, order, space, simplicity, perfection, utility, cleanliness, health, thrift, honesty, permanence and progress.

In a world where so many are working for death, we want to work for life. Working for life means considering other people's lives and needs as important as your own and placing all your efforts and talents at the service of the neediest. This is a profoundly moral choice and, once taken, gives sense to life and action. United and organized, this is an invincible revolutionary force. Jose Marti, speaking for our people, expressed this determination in beautiful and real terms when he wrote, "With the poor people of the earth, I want to share my fate."

Architecture is only one of the physical expressions of life and the values created by the people. Architectural forms and styles alone are meaningless without human content and human value. Architecture must help to produce, within the means available, better persons and a better life for all. Then human unselfishness can be the real style. When the means and resources are in the hands of and at the service of the people, material culture can be considered and organized harmoniously and architecture integrated into the environment.

Human needs form a complex system of interrelationships. They never occur isolated from one another. As they are satisfied, they rise to a more complex level of interaction. That is the process of harmonious human development. By transforming human relationships, architecture, environment, and culture will be consciously transformed. Human relationships are transformed when there is no economic, social or cultural dependence between persons.

The environmental system is the physical frame for human relationships and both together form a unity towards development. Environmental design, as we conceive it, is the art and science of the five senses and the conscience at the service of the people.

A system of human needs corresponds to a system of human functions and activities; to these corresponds a system of spaces both public and private. To these corresponds a human environment in which architecture is of a scale between urbanism and equipment. Technology is an instrument to achieve the satisfaction of material human needs. Form and style are instruments to achieve cultural human needs which are ever developing.

In Cuba, since 1960, a tremendous effort has been made towards creating a truly human environment for all, within our material possibilities. It has been done struggling against years of underdevelopment, aggressions and economic blockade. This effort has been almost completely kept from the American people or presented to them in a deeply distorted image.

This project for a small community has enabled us to engage in a serious and respectful interchange of ideas with students and professors and to express the tone of modernity which is much more than a skin deep modernism. It arises from a sense of tradition and cultural identity, from the values of a new society and creates the human reason for the architecture and the environment of a people sovereign.

**A Diplomatic Mission in
New York City
Lisa Reindorf
Critic: Klaus Herdeg
Third year, spring 1982**

1. Second floor
2. Third floor
3. Exterior perspective

The central issue of the project was creating an image for a foreign country within a neighborhood with a strong architectural character. The traditional pattern along Madison Avenue consists of tall, massive buildings that anchor the ends of the blocks. These buildings have a public zone at street level with a residential block above. The breakdown of the massing at the top of these buildings for gardens and terraces creates an interesting skyline along Madison Avenue.

This neighborhood's character is maintained on the exterior of the building while its image is expressed on the interior in a courtyard/conservatory. Derived from the Spanish courtyard tradition, the conservatory is both the focus of the public functions and a source of light for the building. The public areas—ballroom and library—overlook the conservatory as do offices arranged along one side. The mission entrance is on 75th Street. The consulate section of the building faces the avenue and is organized around a large entrance hall from which the consulate functions are reached.

The staff residences, located above the consulate, overlook either the avenue or the park. Three additional luxury apartments are placed above the mission, but these are terraced to provide outdoor space for the apartments and to maintain the scale of the adjoining house on 75th Street.

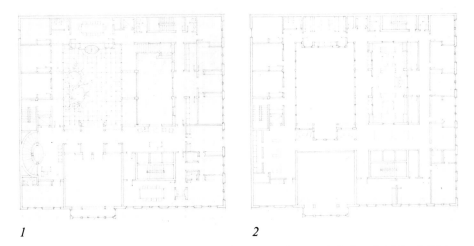

1   *2*

3

4. *Fourth floor*
5. *Fifth—ambassador's residence*
6. *Consulate entrance hall*
7. *East-West section*
8. *North-South section*

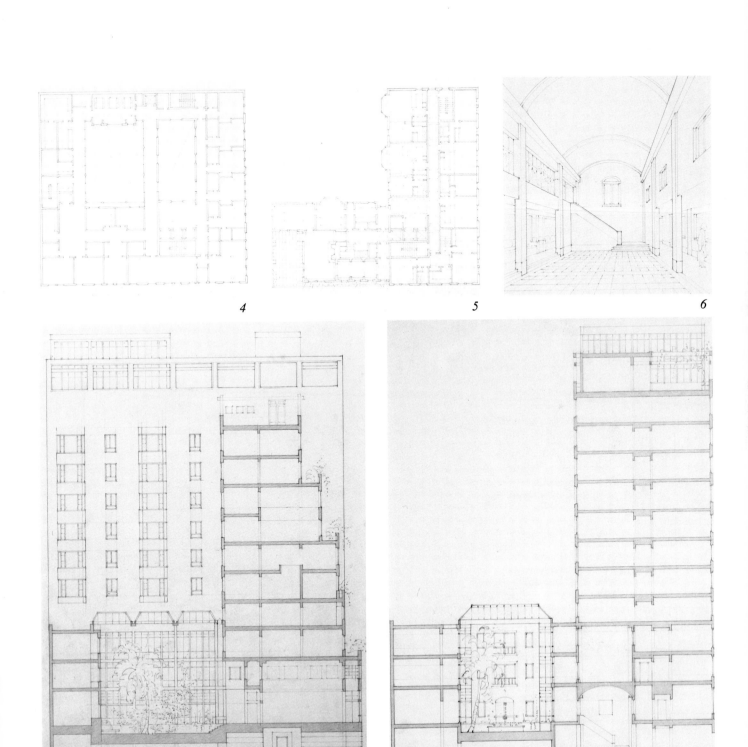

4

5

6

7

8

**A Diplomatic Mission in
New York City
Philippe Dordai
Critic: Klaus Herdeg
Third year, spring 1982**

1. East-west section

The courtyard configuration of this project makes an inwardly-focussed space appropriate to the function of a mission and consulate within a dense urban environment. The general consulate, filling a public function, is placed on the avenue side of the building, below a residential slab. Entry to the consulate is through a three story atrium on the ground floor. Mission functions are on the street side, and are organized around the courtyard which is raised one level from the street. A more understated entrance to the mission doubles as a car drop-off for important guests. A shared reference library on the second floor is the link between the courtyard and the atrium. The corner is occupied by a double-height ballroom that is accessible from either the mission or consulate sides.

The living suites for the ambassador and consul general on the fourth floor make a transition from the courtyard building to the residential slab. The slab rises eight stories above the four stories of the courtyard building to a rooftop swimming pool and sun deck. The placement of the slab responds to adjacent buildings on the avenue which are also twelve to thirteen stories high.

The exterior of the building is treated as a solid wall with punched openings to reinforce the inward-looking nature of the courtyard parti. The courtyard and interior face of the slab are treated with larger openings and balconies. At the point where the slab intersects the courtyard building, a glass wall cascades down and forms the small reading room of the shared library.

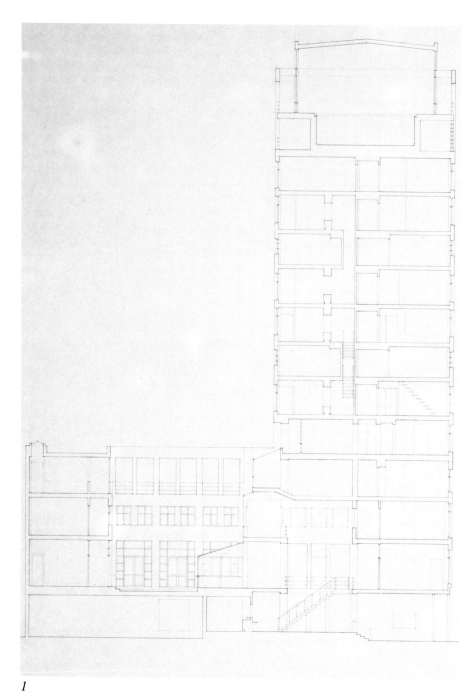

1

2. Second floor plan
3. Typical residential plan
4. Detail of elevation
5. Interior perspective

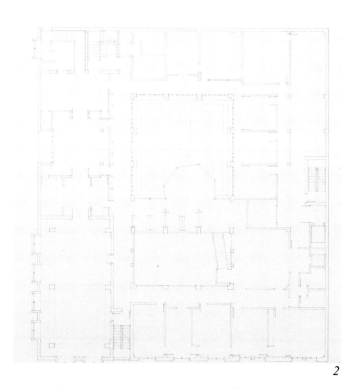

2

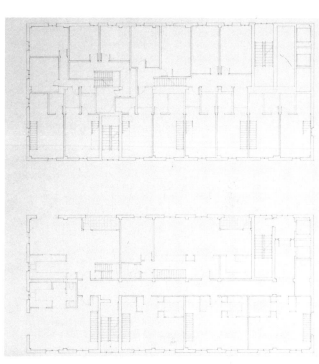

3

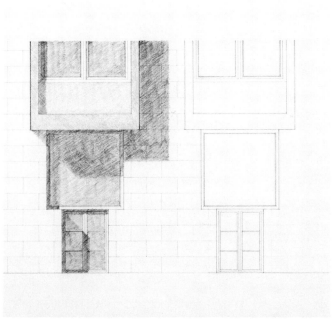

4

5

Mixed-Use Complex
Holly Prenzler
Critic: Ada Karmi-Melamede
Third year, spring 1982

The decision to build on an L-shaped lot facing Third Avenue, between 60th and 61st Streets, permits a high building which can take advantage of the fine views of Central Park to the northwest and the Queensboro Bridge to the southeast. The diagonal of the view orientation, the location of subway access to the southwest and the lot shape prompted me to use the diagonal which bisects the L as an organizing axis. To strengthen this parti, I brought an interior sidewalk, a shortcut, through the site, perpendicular to the subway access below and the major entrance on grade.

I organized a hierarchy of spaces within each functional area of the multi-use building through manipulation of the massing and section. An atrium, double-height offices and living rooms allow floors to interact, creating neighborhoods within the towers.

As part of an historic district, the rowhouses facing 60th and 61st Streets enclose an intriguing and picturesque backyard. A garden pavilion, containing special spaces for each of the building's functions, affords everyone a view into the gardens at the heart of the block. Shoppers can escape to a quiet room and contemplate the garden. Double-height conference rooms for the office floors overlook the trees. The library for apartment dwellers is located on the pavilion's top floor, adjacent to the landscaped roof of the office block, shared by tenants.

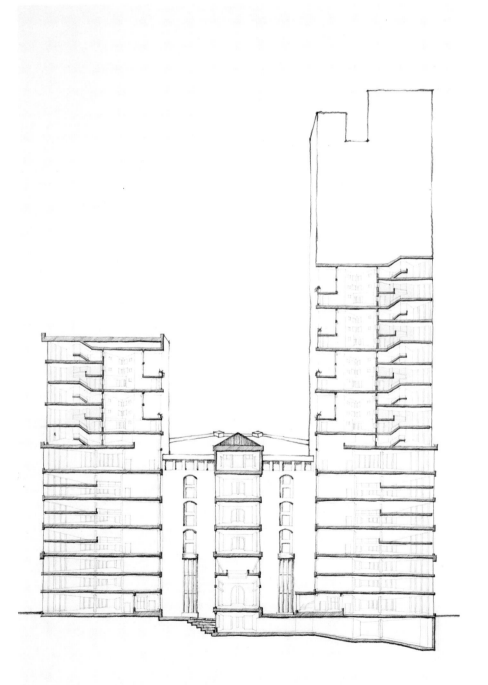

1

2. *Subway level plan*
3. *Ground floor plan*
4. *Typical apartment plan*
5. *Ground floor axonometric*

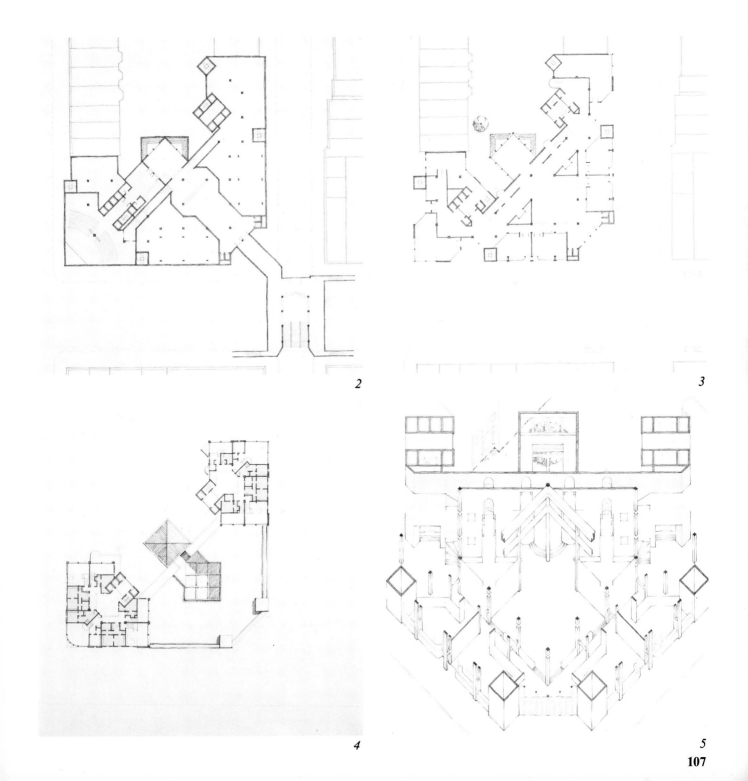

2

3

4

5

Mixed-Use Complex
Robert Lane
Critic: Ada Karmi-Melamede
Third year, spring 1982

1. North-South section
2. Exploded axonometric—lobby
3. First floor plan
4. Exterior perspective

The standard, stacked model for mixed-use development fails to resolve the conflict of unrelated uses, unlike the traditional street.

This project accepts this conflict by providing two towers—one for housing and one for offices. Each has its own center and identity and each meets the street in its own way. The connection of the two towers is resolved by a large, public room. This room, which contains commercial and exhibition spaces, becomes more public as it reaches the intersection, where subway connections and views down the avenue and 60th Street come into play.

The two tower idea enables the building to be frontal to the avenue, but also asymmetrical, reflecting the role of 60th Street as an edge between commercial midtown and the largely residential Upper East Side.

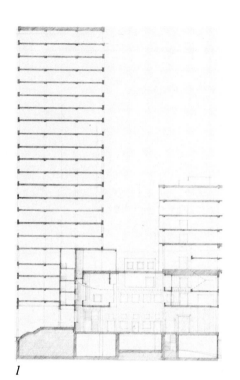

1

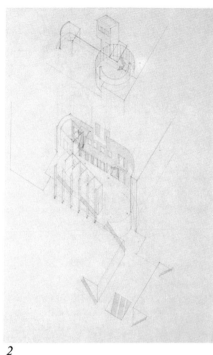

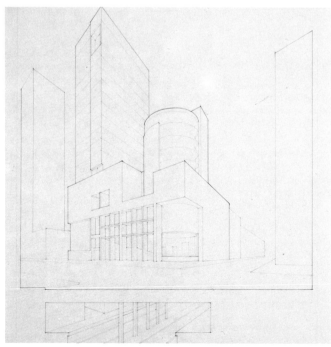

2

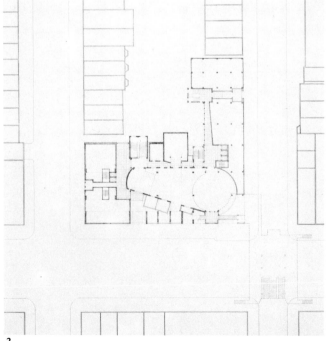

3

4

1. *East-West section*
2. *Avenue elevation*
3. *First floor plan*
4. *Lobby perspective*

Mixed Use Complex
Thomas Brashares
Critic: Ada Karmi-Melamede
Third year, spring 1982

Respect for the street line and typical avenue building height and a desire to open the corners of the block as major circulation points influenced this project. The building has a stone-clad base of offices and commercial space, with two glass housing towers rising from this existing-height base. The towers of housing maximize window area and create twin beacons on the skyine, similar to the San Remo apartments on Manhattan's West Side.

The other important issue in this project involved the public atrium and its relationship to the commercial activities such as the three theaters. I opened the building up to the green of the backyard spaces belonging to the adjacent row houses at the back of the site and layered circulation and structure from the hard edge of Third Avenue to the soft, green backyards.

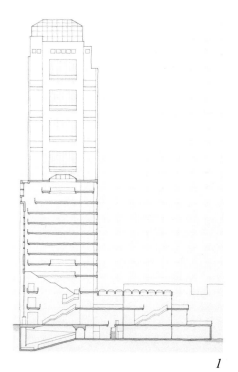

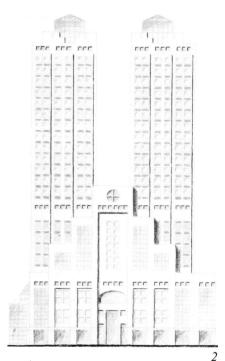

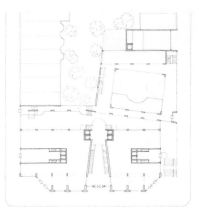

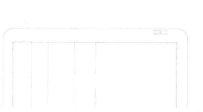

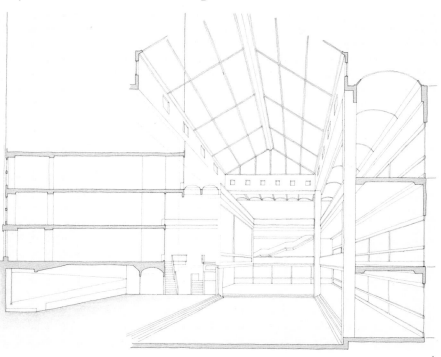

1

2

3

4

Shakertown Visitors Center
Pleasant Hill, Kentucky
Theresa Beyer
Critic: Michael Mostoller
Third year, spring 1982

1. Gallery perspective
2. Upper and lower plans

The Shaker village has become a museum, and so my museum reflects the village. Its linear organization echoes that of the village. Its square bays reflect the Shaker belief in the beauty of perfect forms, even at the expense of utility. Each square bay is divided into one large central bay and eight smaller ones, just as each large family dwelling house is surrounded by smaller outbuildings. The "Big Room" is the equivalent of the Meeting House. In the village, the Meeting House is the only building directly across the street from another building. The "Big Room" in the Visitors' Center is the only room open to both levels, and the only room which contains a room. This room within a room is skewed with respect to the grid of Shakertown and is a place to both escape the grid and to become more aware of its insistence. A second skewed room at the mid-point of the ramps provides an oblique view of the village.

The building is constructed using a modern vernacular. Concrete blocks replace bricks and stones; painted steel studs are used instead of pegboards; curtain walls coexist with punched windows.

The museum is situated just south of the graveyard. One begins one's journey where the Shakers ended theirs. At the far side of the village is a small cafeteria which distinguishes itself from the nearby Shaker buildings by its relationship to their grid. The village is bracketed by the two new buildings, emphasizing the entire village as the Visitors' Center.

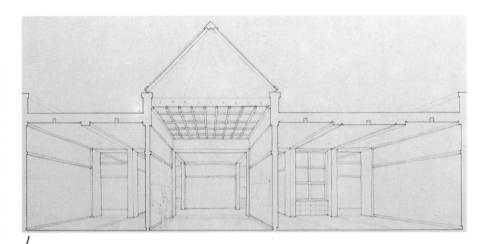

1

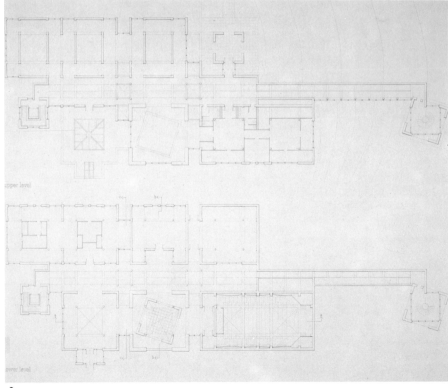

2

3. North and south elevations
4. The big room
5. Cafeteria plan
6. West and south cafeteria elevations

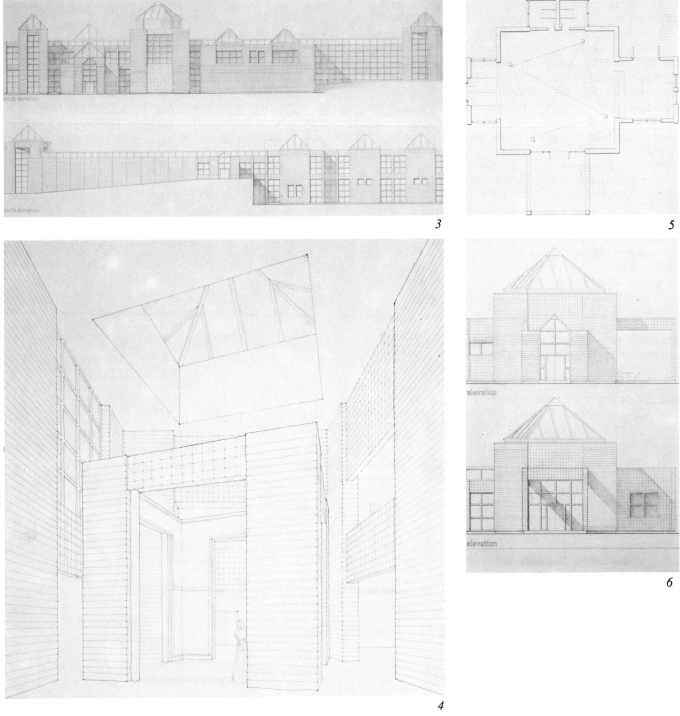

3

5

4

6

Delaware County Office Building
Preservation of the Gordon Villa
Anne E. Weber
Critic: Michael Mostoller
Third year, spring 1982

The Delaware County Courthouse Square in Delhi, New York is a remarkable group of nineteenth century civic, religious, commercial and residential buildings, dominated by the courthouse which was completed in 1867. In the 1970's, the county began to need more administrative office space than this dignified structure could provide. The county acquired the site of the Gordon Villa, directly opposite the courthouse, in 1977 and began plans predicated on the destruction of this Italianate villa of 1856.

My thesis explores a way of saving the villa and reusing it as a part of an office complex. The protection of the architectural integrity of both the courthouse square and the villa itself is the major issue. The office building is placed behind the villa so that its scale, texture and color set off the villa and relate to the other buildings on the square. I used the villa as one of three major blocks of the new office complex connected by lower linking buildings. The main entrance is from the parking lot. This reorientation of approach permits the new building to form a background for the villa and the square and to assume an identity of its own.

In the summer of 1982, the injunction against demolition, which had been obtained by Delhi residents, was dissolved. The building which dominated the south side of the square and balanced the courthouse was destroyed.

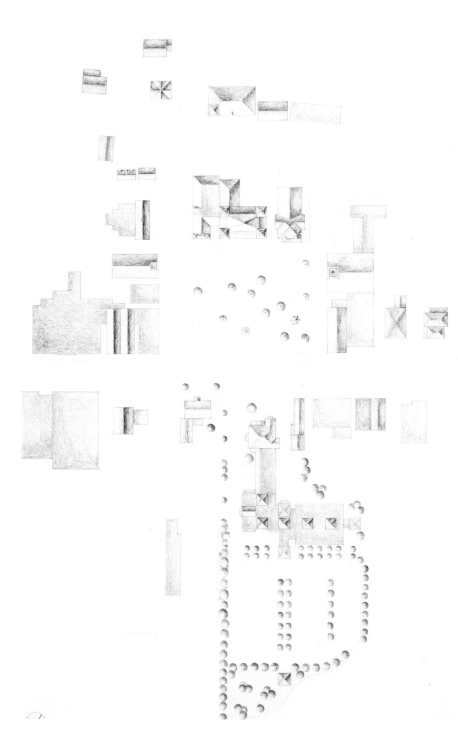

2. *West elevation*
3. *First floor plan*
4. *Elevation detail: entrance*

GORDON VILLA

2

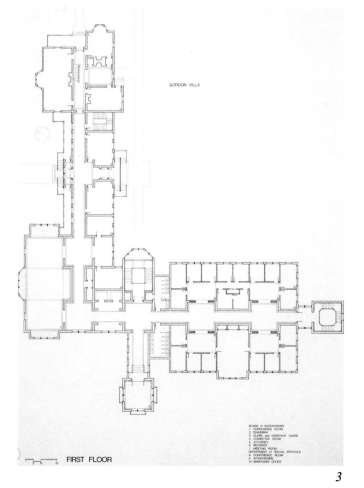

GORDON VILLA

FIRST FLOOR

BOARD of SUPERVISORS
1. CONFERENCE ROOM
2. CHAIRMAN
3. CLERK and ASSISTANT CLERK
4. COMMITTEE ROOM
5. ATTORNEY
6. RECORDS
7. MEETING ROOM
DEPARTMENT of SOCIAL SERVICES
8. CONFERENCE ROOM
9. INTERVIEWING
10. MANPOWER OFFICE

3

DELAWARE COUNTY

4

Community for 5000 Inhabitants, Cuba
Peter Anders, Neil McNulty and Geoffery Moore
Critics: Fernando Salinas, Roberto Segre and Michel Kagan
Third year, spring 1982

1. Site axonometric
2. Site plan

Lenin Park lies to the south of Havana bordered on the east by a dam and on the west by the old highway to Havana. Parallel to this road is the site of an industrial city for five thousand people. The city was designed based on the principle of shared activities and spaces. The decentralized nature of the community is a response to Cuban ideology and a reaction to the alienating abstraction of modern urbanism.

The "face" of the city is a long wall of housing and services which parallels the tree-lined highway. Faster traffic is rerouted around the city so that the highway becomes its boulevard. In the tradition of communist city plans of the twenties, the city is linear to span between neighboring towns. Its walls act as a gateway for Lenin Park's visitors. The city's orientation results from the need for ventilation.

The town is made up of five districts, each with its own plaza and social center. These centers are, from north to south: a cultural center, a market, a school and museum, a recreation center, and a food processing plant.

Low perimeter-block housing surrounds the plazas. These units serve families and the elderly. The principle of shared space allows the occupant of the city to dwell simultaneously in a court, a plaza and a district. This is accomplished by a multitude of scales and a weaving of enclosures.

The entire city is split horizontally by a datum which occurs at the roof level of the low housing. This break allows wind passage and its surface provides a cool retreat in the evenings. It also introduces another pedestrian path through the city.

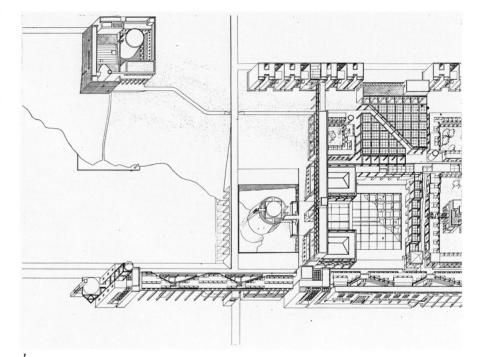

1

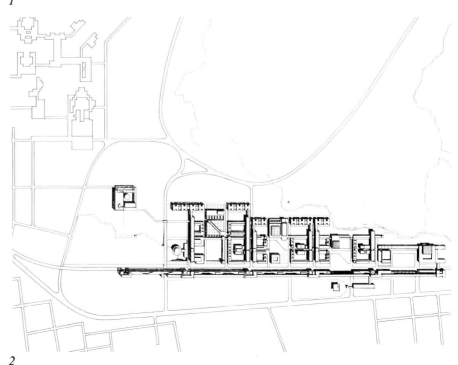

2

3. Diagrams

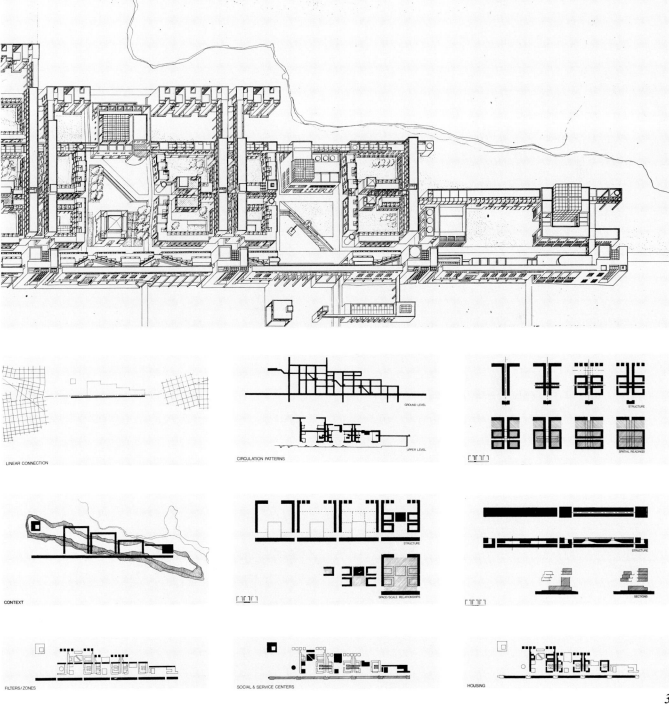

LINEAR CONNECTION

CIRCULATION PATTERNS

GROUND LEVEL

UPPER LEVEL

STRUCTURE

SPATIAL READINGS

CONTEXT

STRUCTURE

SPACE/SCALE RELATIONSHIPS

STRUCTURE

SECTIONS

FILTERS/ZONES

SOCIAL & SERVICE CENTERS

HOUSING

Community for 5000 Inhabitants, Cuba
James Durfee and Joseph Lloyd
Critics: Fernando Salinas, Roberto Segre and Michel Kagan
Third year, spring 1982

1. Site axonometric

Situated in a suburban park of Havana, the city for 5,000 people has two natural edges: a small lake and a hill rising up from it. The project attempts to reinforce the latter edge by presenting a "wall" building to the outside which defines the limit of the new community and expresses its collective nature. Two major elements, a factory and a cultural center, punctuate the ends of this edge. The third major element, a school, is placed in a strong relationship to the factory and is connected to the cultural center by a diagonal pedestrian street leading up the hill.

In the large triangular piazza between the street top of the hill, major recreational, political, and commercial activities are provided for, with a large open-air market as its central piece. Forming the lakeside edge of the diagonal street, L-shaped residential blocks are oriented towards the water. From these, lines of housing extend down the hill progressing from an urban context through a natural landscape and ending at the water's edge.

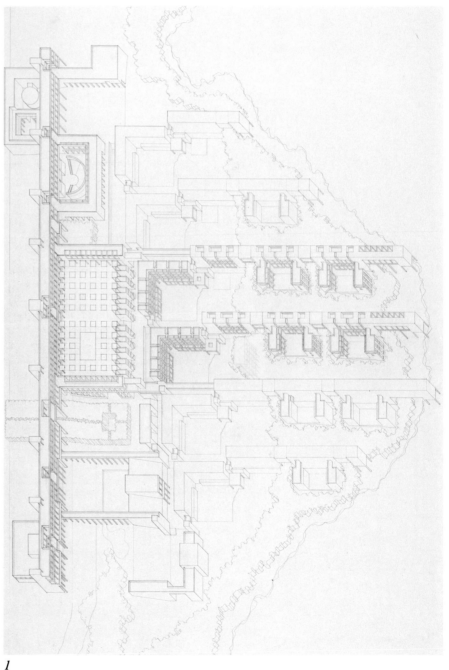

1

2. *First, second and fourth floor*
   plans
3. *Site plan*
4. *Housing section*
5. *Diagrams*

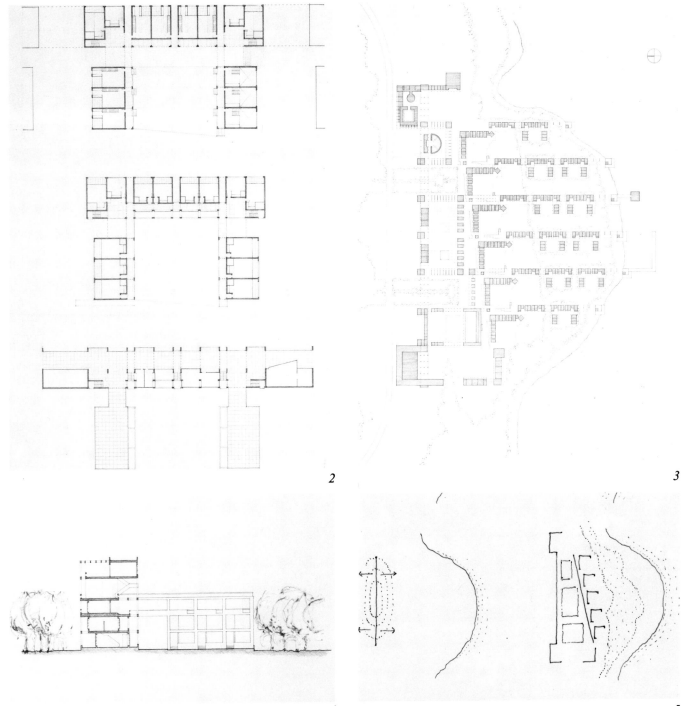

2

3

4

5

**Historic Preservation
Master of Science
Spring 1982**

The Spring Studio for first year Historic Preservation students focuses on problems of preservation architecture or preservation planning. South Street Seaport, The Brooklyn Bridge, Chinatown, and the nineteenth century commercial area of Ladies Mile have at one time or another all been the subject of study. In the case of South Street Seaport, students have questioned the impact of new commercial development on this historic area, the problems of recycling and rehabilitating vacated structures, the issues of authenticity with respect to historic reconstruction and adaptive re-use. When a case such as Ladies Mile is the focus of study, the intention has been to analyze historically the nineteenth century development of the commercial area, to present graphically the sedimented layers of its past development, its building types, the evolution of its block and lot structure, its shifting urbanistic qualities, and to evaluate its potential as a future Historic District.

The purpose of this studio is to draw upon a series of skills developed by all students in the first semester studio and to apply them in a comprehensive manner to a New York City preservation project. Thus analysis of Building Department records and Real Estate conveyances, the development of land-use plans and the study of nineteenth century insurance maps and city directories become the basis for a proposed preservation plan. The evaluation of design guidelines for infill structures in Historic Districts, techniques of intervention in the built environment, the analysis of historic materials and building technologies become the basis for new designs by the preservation architects.

Christine Boyer

1. *Blake: Plan and perspective*
2. *Blake: Elevations*
3. *Larson and Pellar*

Hugh O'Neill Building Storefront
Dennis Blake
Catherine Larson and Nina Pellar
Critic: Robert Meadows
First year, spring 1982

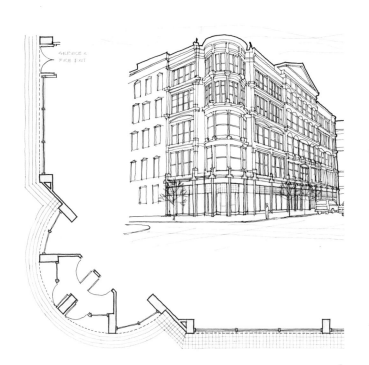

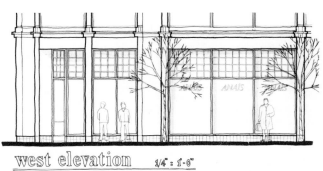

west elevation   1/4" : 1'-0"

south elevation   1/4" : 1'-0"

1

2

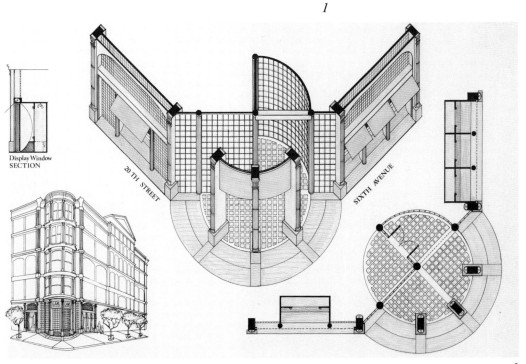

Display Window
SECTION

20 TH STREET

SIXTH AVENUE

3

Urban Design
Master of Science
Fall 1981
Spring 1982

There was a time when architects were more involved in designing cities. They thought of architecture in terms of streetwalls. They related their building designs to buildings by others. They used their designs to create and advance larger plans and purposes that involved more than a single building. They were interested in the nature of a place, and therefore, spent time considering and relating to existing conditions. These were used as a basis for design.

Buildings, consequently, were influenced as much from outside forces as from interior user needs. Often the outside forces of context, place and street were more important form determinants than the functions inside. Form did not necessarily follow function. These architects did not call themselves urban designers. They practiced urban design as an integral part of their profession.

The objective of the Urban Design program is to rediscover and redefine the traditional attitudes and skills of the architect. The result, we hope, is that urban designers can once again be called architects.

Columbia University's Urban Design program trains architects to be active and effective participants in the urban development process. Students are introduced to the point of view that urban designers design and that their client is the public. Designing for the public, rather than for 'user needs', is a kind of culture shock for most of the incoming class. The public client requires the designer to see things as a whole and in a large context.

The Urban Design curriculum presumes that physical form is not an accident. The philosophy of the program is that urban design recommendations should build upon existing physical relationships rather than impose pre-conceived solutions which disrupt such relationships. The combination of natural features and man-made policies shape the environment and determine the course of development.

The curriculum also focuses on pragmatic, analytic and technical skills. Consequently, exposure to other disciplines—law, real estate economics and implementation—is mandatory.

As in architectural education, the design studio is the core of the Urban Design program. Among the issues addressed are land use and physical development, large scale development, circulation systems, implementation strategies, and public benefits (which are the objectives of any urban design effort).

The fall studio introduces tools and techniques through a series of brief problems at different scales. The first problem requires map analysis and the interpretation of the city's component systems. Through the production of a city-wide land use strategy, this project acquaints students with the way a city functions, with the regular patterns and form of a city, and explains how places are unique because of their location.

The next project, local area analysis, reveals the program's bias that each and every place in a city demands its own particular plan and physical expression. As with all studio problems, this one expands the students' vocabulary and graphic ability to describe the physical parts and systems of a city. Understanding what exists is not a mechanical or a descriptive process. It is highly subjective and results in the student's formulation of a vision of what the place wants to be.

The final fall studio problem involves the analysis and redesign of an existing, significant public place in each student's local area. This problem focuses on a smaller scale group of independently owned buildings that enclose and establish a public space. The problem reveals the potential for individual buildings to be designed as part of a larger whole and when the design of a single building is of secondary importance to the design of the larger public space.

The spring studio incorporates the lessons learned in the fall studio by applying them to a major urban development problem that is concurrently under review in New York City. The design problems in the fall term are primarily concerned with physical considerations. The spring studio problem also includes political, economic, and implementation considerations as well as their impact on the physical design.

Stanton Eckstut

1. *Existing conditions*
2. *Concept*
3. *Site axonometric*

23rd Street Landing
Joy Cuming
Critic: Stanton Eckstut
Urban Design, spring 1982

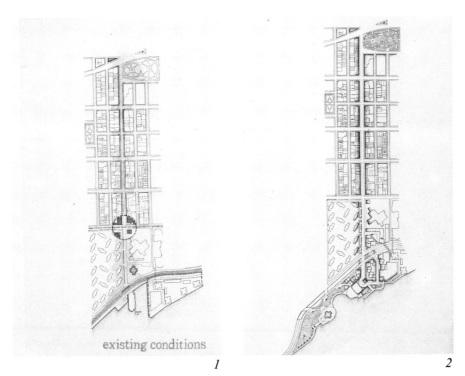

existing conditions

1

2

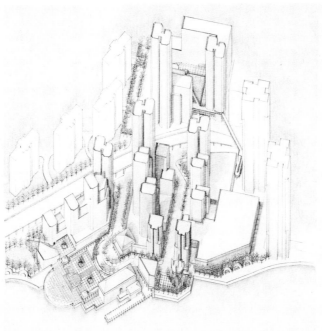

East 23rd Street begins where Broadway crosses Manhattan's grid to produce Madison Square. Between this public park and First Avenue, the corridor of East 23rd Street reinforces the square's significance by maintaining a continuous street wall and a consistent scale, density, frontage width and architectural order.

East of First Avenue, the streetwall of East 23rd is interrupted by individual object-type housing buildings. The blocks are larger, breaking the rhythm of the grid. The developments are introverted and dilute the street life. The public is not drawn to the natural end of the street because its directionality is diffused. The barrier created by the large blocks is exaggerated by FDR Drive, an elevated highway which separates Manhattan from the East River waterfront.

An important architectural landmark is the bathhouse at the intersection of 23rd Street and FDR Drive. The incidental nature of its surroundings weakens its prominence; the overgrown park in which it stands is perceived as a hole in the streetscape rather than a pause in a comprehensible pattern of solids and voids. In order to unify the area, the bathhouse is moved and the void is filled with a built form which respects the vocabulary of the street and reinstates the plane of the streetwall. This helps to screen FDR Drive and extend the street to the unobstructed shoreline.

The new progression of East 23rd Street is from a well-regulated corridor which opens up and steps down to an urban plaza. From the plaza, the view across a sheltered cove to a public park centers on the classical bathhouse, an historical symbol of 23rd Street.

3

Bowling Green Development
Carol Senft
Critic: Stanton Eckstut
Urban Design, fall 1981

The intention of this proposal is to indicate the potential for future growth and maintain the desirable features of the Bowling Green and United States Custom House area. This site, in the financial district of lower Manhattan, is significant as the southern terminus of Broadway, the city's longest street. At a smaller scale, the site is unique because of the nature of the forms creating this terminus—Bowling Green, one of the few sizable open spaces in the area, and the landmark Customs House.

In order to balance the pragmatism of urban analysis (of topography, transportation, edges) with formal investigations, several criteria for growth in the area are proposed. An increased degree of closure for the Customs House would help to distinguish Bowling Green from Battery Park. Setbacks in new buildings surrounding the green respond to and help resolve the changes in the street grid.

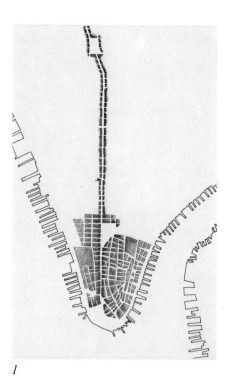

1

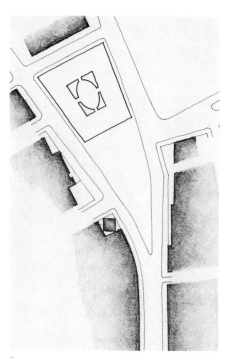

2

3

4

1. *Site plan*
2. *Vistas at Sheridan Square*
3. *Existing: Grove Street from
   W. 4th Street*
4. *Proposed: Grove Street from
   W. 4th Street*
5. *Existing: Square from
   7th Avenue*
6. *Proposed: Square from
   7th Avenue*

Sheridan Square, Greenwich Village
Eve Picker
Critic: Stanton Eckstut
Urban Design, fall 1981

This project involved a detailed analysis which established the important physical characteristics of the area and required a redevelopment proposal for substantially increased floor area. Four sites at the western end of the square, where Seventh Avenue had destroyed the basic structure of the Village street and block grid, were recommended for redevelopment. Urban design guidelines were based on several issues:

1) enclosure—an increase in bulk around the square at its western end reinforces its importance.

2) termination of vistas—enhancement of street terminations and placement of a landmark and gateways emphasizes the sense of arrival for pedestrians and motorists.

3) continuity of scale—consideration must be given to height, bulk, fenestration, land use and ornamentation.

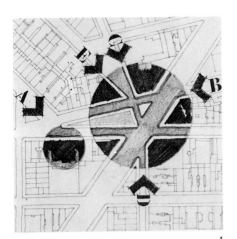

1

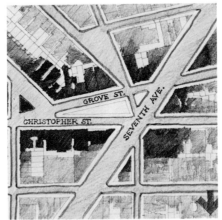

2

3

4

5

6

**Esquisse: Memorial for the Vietnam
Veterans of New York City
Ray Porfilio
Marcus Gleysteen
Critic: Timothy Wood
Second year, spring 1982**

1. *Porfilio: Plan*
2. *Porfilio: Perspective*
3. *Gleysteen: Plan*
4. *Gleysteen: Perspective and section*

Porfilio: The memorial is located in Battery Park on the axis between Bowling Green and the Statue of Liberty. Bowling Green represents an act of civilization, the first setting aside of land for shared public use in New York. The Statue of Liberty captures those values for which people sacrifice. Within the park, the Fort and the New Amsterdam Flagpole, align with the elements outside. The proposed memorial reinforces the axis through two tree-lined promenades running from the flagpole to the Fort. A terrace flanked by coniferous trees is introduced between the promenades. The terrace is divided by a shallow trough in which the names of those who lost their lives are inscribed and water flows.

Gleysteen: Memorial at Liberty Plaza, Lower Manhattan.

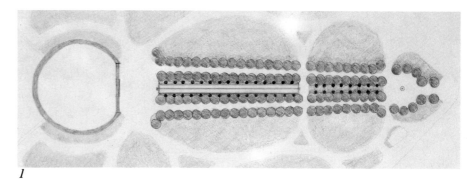

1

2

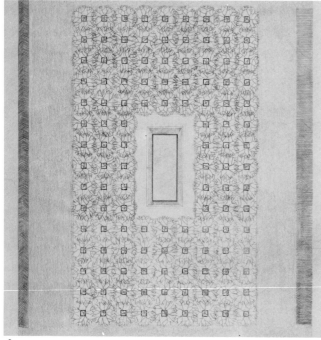

3

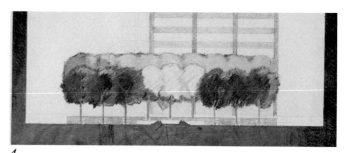

4

1. Gerber: Elevation
2. Wax: Axonometric

Alan Gerber
Critic: Susana Torre
Donna Wax
Critic: Steven Holl

1

Gerber: Memorial Bridge spanning East 42nd Street at Tudor City.

Wax: This New York City memorial symbolizes the contradictions and ironies of the Vietnam Era through the manipulation of a known type, the war memorial bridge. The existing Canal Street Bridge, a remnant left by the demolition of the West Side Highway, stands connecting nothing and spanning nothing. The intersection of it with another free-standing bridge creates a depiction of the conflict between old and new, the irony of a lack of historical context and a negation of the victory traditionally symbolized. At the bridges' crossing, marble slabs are inscribed with the names of the New York City residents who died. Standing on the old bridge, one can look out to the city and the water, a symbol of hope.

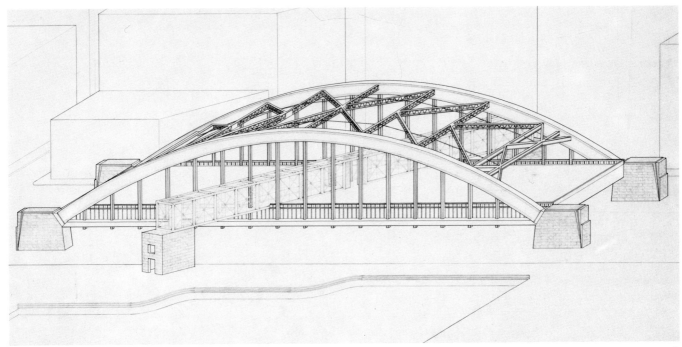

2

P.A. Morton
Critic: Steven Holl

1. Morton: Perspective to east
2. Morton: Perspective to west
3. Morton: Axonometric

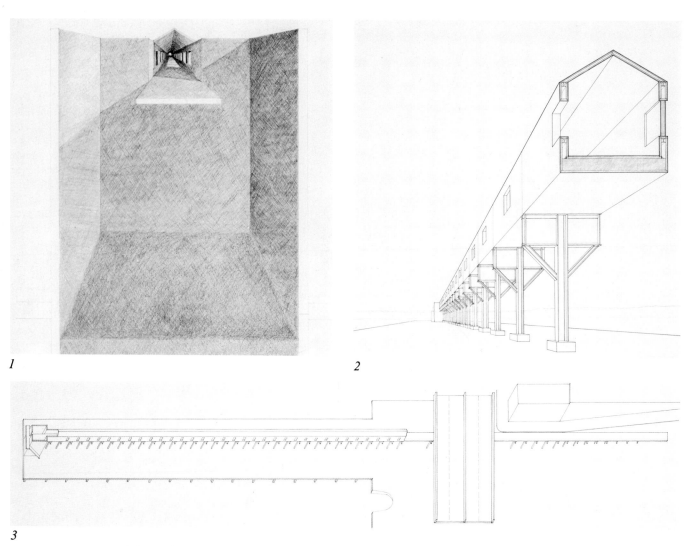

1

2

3

Morton: Memorial on Pier 97 at 57th Street

This is a memorial to celebrate the end of the war. Our collective guilt about the Vietnam war cannot be visited on those who died, who fought and were wounded or psychologically maimed, those who did what we asked of them. This memorial is to honor those who served us and died doing so.

1. Griffin: Perspective
2. Keenen: Axonometric

William Griffin
Critic: Robert A.M. Stern
John Keenen
Critic: Steven Holl

Griffin: Memorial at Park Avenue and Ninety-Sixth Street.

Keenen: By use of simple materials and techniques, an abandoned pier on Manhattan's West Side is transformed into an Anti-War Memorial of Remembrance. "Walls" of white sailcloth are suspended from iron girders. The visitor advances through increasingly larger "doorways". Light enters the silent pier only through skylights, and the open end of the pier. The wind from the river races through the empty pier, causing the fabric walls to sway and rustle. At the end of the pier, one is confronted with the force of falling water. The silence experienced at the beginning of the pier is shattered; a final bay is seen partially submerged, the white sailcloth walls wavering in the wind.

1

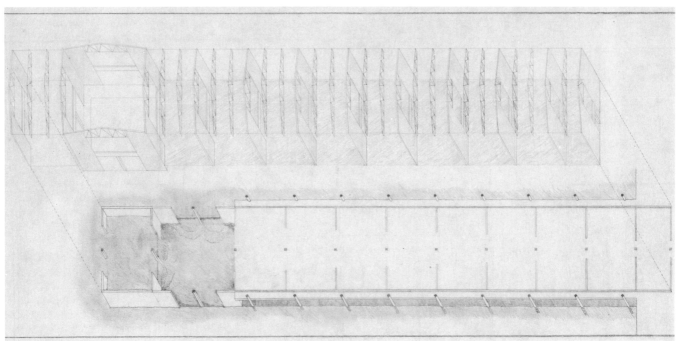

2

Photographic Credits

8 Courtesy of Richard Sexton/Matrix Photographics

9 Courtesy of Max Protetch Gallery, 37 West 57th Street, New York, NY

10 Courtesy of *Lotus* 17, 1977, p. 104

Courtesy of Design Collaborative

11 Courtesy of Tim Street-Porter

12 Courtesy of *Global Architecture Document 1970-80,* 1980

13 Courtesy of Robert A.M. Stern

14 Courtesy of Johnson/Burgee Architects

Courtesy of Murphy/Jahn Architects

15 Courtesy of *Global Architecture House 10,* March, 1982

16 Courtesy of Daniel Monk

18, 19, 20, 21 Theresa Gordon Beyer

22 *1. and 2.* Atlas Portland Cement Co., New York, 1907

23 *3. Deutscher Werkbund Yearbook,* 1913
4. Le Corbusier, *Vers Une Architecture,* 1922

24 *Deutscher Werkbund Yearbook,* 1913

25 Le Corbusier, *L'Esprit Nouveau,* 1920

26 Benevolo, Leonardo, *The History of Modern Architecture,* MIT Press, 1977

27 Guinness, Desmond, *Mr. Jefferson Architect,* The Viking Press, 1973, p. 126

28 *The Architectural Review,* July, 1936. Courtesy of Avery Library, Columbia University

29, 30, 31 Courtesy of Avery Library, Columbia University

32 *1. Abacus The Museum of Finish Architecture Yearbook,* 1979, p. 91
2. Abacus, p. 84
3. Loja Saarinen in *Eliel Saarinen* by Albert Christ-Janer, University of Chicago Press, 1979, p. 18

33 *4.* Christ-Janer, pp. 14 and 15
5. Christ-Janer, p. 13
6. F.J. Kidder in Christ-Janer, p. 25
7. Christ-Janer, p. 13

34 *8.* Christ-Janer, p. 24
9. Eric Sundstrom in Christ-Janer, p. 31

35 *10.* Christ-Janer, p. 66
11. Courtesy of *Architectural Record,* December 1930, p. 448

36, 37, 38, 39 Courtesy of Steven Holl

40 *1. Building Age,* June, 1920, p. 51

41 *2.* Ford, James, *America's Little House,* Better Homes in America, Inc., New York, 1934, title page

42 *3. and 4. The New York Times,* May 4, 1919, Real Estate, p. 2
5., 6. and 7. Courtesy of *Architectural Record,* July 1920, pp. 27 and 69

43 *8. Stein, Clarence, Towards New Towns in America,* MIT Press, 1957, p. 25
9. and 10. Courtesy of *Architectural Record,* July 1920, pp. 59 and 58

48 *1.* Rowe, Colin, *The Mathematics of the Ideal Villa.* MIT Press, 1978
2. Christ, Ivan, *Le Louvre et Les Tuileries,* Edition "Tel", 1949, p. 111

49 *3.* Benevolo, Leonardo, *The History of Modern Architecture,* MIT Press, 1977, p. 153
4. Le Corbusier, *Oeuvre Complete, 1934-38,* p. 143

60, 61, 62, 63 Courtesy of Michael Mostoller